A-GONG'S TABLE

A Chez Jorge Cookbook

A-GONG'S
TABLE

Vegan Recipes from a Taiwanese Home

GEORGE LEE

Photographs by LAURENT HSIA

TEN SPEED PRESS
California | New York

Contents

Introduction 1
  A Note About Language 5

The Larder 9

Condiments 10
  xiānggūfěn / Mushroom Powder 15
  làjiāojiàng / Fermented Chili Paste 16
  tiánlàjiàng / Sweet Chili Sauce 17
  tángsuàn / Pickled Garlic 18

Dry Goods 24

Spices 26
  wǔxiāng / Five-Spice 27
  shísānxiāng / Thirteen-Spice 27

Equipment 28

Preserved Vegetables 30
  suāncài | kiâm-tshài / Fermented Mustard Greens 35
  xuěcài | sin-kiâm-tshài / Preserved Greens 41
  tshài-póo / Preserved Radish 42
  jiàngdōngguā | tang-kue-tsiùnn / Winter Melon in Soybean Sauce 45
  jiàngguā | tsiùnn-kue-á / Cucumbers in Sweet Soy Sauce 47
  yìnguā | ìm-kue-á / Oriental Pickling Melons in White Soy Sauce 49
  jiàngfènglí | ông-lâi-tsiùnn / Pineapple in Soybean Sauce 50
  tiánjiǔ dòufǔrǔ | tāu-lú / Sweet Wine Fermented Bean Curd 52

Vegetarian Meat 54
  miànjīn | mī-thi / Wheat Gluten 56
  miàncháng | mī-tsià / Gluten Intestine 58
  písī / Gluten Threads 59
  miànjīnpào / Gluten Puffs 60
  dòujī / Soy Chicken 61
  hóutóugū | kâu-thâu-koo / Lion's Mane Mushrooms 62

Breakfast 64

  han-tsî-bê / Sweet Potato Congee 67
  tǔdòu miànjīn | thôo-tāu-mī-thi / Braised Gluten with Peanuts 68
  dòujiāng | tāu-ni / Soy Milk 74
  xiándòujiāng | kiâm-tāu-ni / Savory Soy Milk 77
  mǐjiāng | bí-tsiunn / Peanut Rice Milk 78
  xìngrénchá | hīng-lîn tê / Almond Tea 79
  dànbǐng | nn̄g-piánn / Egg Crepes 81
  shāobǐng | sio-piánn / Sesame Flatbread 82
  yóutiáo | iû-tsiah-ké / Fried Crullers 85
  fàntuán | pn̄g-uân / Sticky Rice Roll 88
  xiāngchūn zhuābǐng / Flaky Toon Pancakes 91
  májiàngmiàn / Sesame Noodles 93
    làyóu / Chili Oil 95

Little Eats 96

  sūzhà dòubāo / Crispy Fried Tofu Skin 101
    táishì pàocài / Pickled Cabbage 103
  guàbāo | kuah-pau / Gua Bao 104
    chǎosuāncài / Stir-Fried Mustard Greens 107
  ô-á-tsian / Oyster Omelet 108
  uánn-kué / Bowl Rice Cake 111
  xiánsūgū | kiâm-soo-koo / Popcorn Mushrooms 113
    zǐcàigāo | tì-huī-kué / Purple Laver Cake 115
  lǔwèi / Soy-Braised Goods 116
  lǜdòu yìrén | lik-tāu-ì-lîn / Mung Bean Soup with Pearl Barley 119
  dòuhuā | tāu-hue / Tofu Pudding with Stewed Peanuts and Sweet Red Beans 121

Vegetables 126

  liángsǔn / Bamboo Salad 129
  huángjīn pàocài / Golden Kimchi 130

méizì xiǎofānqié / Plum Pickled Cherry Tomatoes 132

tàng dìguāyè / Blanched Sweet Potato Leaves 135

fǔrǔ kōngxīncài / Water Spinach with Fermented Bean Curd 136

fānqié huāyécài / Tomato and Cauliflower Stir-Fry 139

xuěcài dòugān / Preserved Greens and Bean Curd Stir-Fry 140

jiāngsī càiguā | kiunn-si tshài-kue / Loofah Stir-Fried with Ginger 143

tǎxiāng qiézi / Basil-Fragrant Eggplants 144

Soups 146

gāotāng | bú-thng / All-Purpose Stock 150

shàngtāng / Superior Stock 151

zhúsǔntāng | tik-sún-thng / Bamboo Soup 153

liánǒutāng | liân-ngāu-thng / Lotus Root Soup 154

dōngguā wánzitāng / Winter Melon Soup with Tofu Balls 156

fènglí kǔguātāng | ông-lâi-khóo-kue-thng / Pineapple and Bitter Melon Soup 159

sìshéntāng | sù-sîn-thng / Four Tonics Soup 160

hóngshāomiàn | âng-sio-mi / Beef Noodle Soup 161

mǐfěnyù | bí-hún-ōo / Taro Rice Noodle Soup 165

miànxiàngēng | mī-suànn-kôo / Mee Sua 168

Mains 171

sùlǔfàn | sòo-lóo-pñg / Braised Pork over Rice 173

yóucōng | iû-tshang / Fried Shallots 175

méigāncài sùzào / Minced Pork with Aged Mustard Greens 176

sǔnsī | sún-si / Braised Bamboo Shoots 179

hóngqú chǎofàn | âng-khak-tshá-pñg / Red Yeast Fried Rice 180

gālǐfàn | ka-lí-pñg / Curry Rice 182

gāolìcài fàn | ko-lê-tshài-pñg / Cabbage Rice 184

tshài-póo-nñg / Preserved Radish Omelet 187

yìnchǐ dòufǔ | ìm-sīnn-tāu-hū / Black Bean Tofu 188

báicàilǔ | pe̍h-tshài-lóo / Napa Cabbage Stew 191

sānbēi hóutóugū / Three Cup Lion's Mane Mushrooms 195

jīnguā mǐfěnchǎo | kim-kue bí-hún-tshá / Pumpkin Fried Rice Noodles 196

wǔliǔjū | ngóo-liú-ki / Five Willow Fried Fish 197

málà huǒguō / Mala Hot Pot 205

málà guōdǐ / Mala Base 208

jiāngmǔguō | kiunn-bú-ko / Herbal Ginger Hot Pot 209

máyóu miànxiàn | muâ-iû-mī-suànn / Sesame Oil Vermicelli 212

Festival and Food 215

yóufàn | iû-pñg / Taiwanese Sticky Rice 220

fótiàoqiáng / Buddha Jump over the Wall 223

chángniáncài tāng | tn̂g-nî-tshài-thng / Long-Life Mustard Greens Soup 225

niángāo | tinn-kué / New Year Rice Cake 231

luóbogāo | tshài-thâu-kué / Turnip Cake 234

yùwán | ōo-uân / Fried Taro Balls 237

rùnbǐng | jūn-piánn / Popiah Rolls 238

kinn-tsàng / Alkaline Rice Dumplings 243

dòushā | tāu-se / Sweet Red Bean Paste 245

hēizhīmá tāngyuán | oo-muâ-înn-á / Glutinous Rice Balls with Black Sesame 247

jiǔniàng | tsiú-tinn / Sweet Fermented Rice 249

Acknowledgments 250

Index 251

Introduction

A-Gong, my paternal grandpa, was an architect. After my mom had my brother and me, he built a wooden house for us to grow up in. The house nestled at the foot of a mountain near Tamsui River, on the outskirts of Taipei, where trees were black in the night and our whispers hid behind deciduous leaves. With most of Taipei facing the seismic shifts that came with modernization, Tamsui seemed frozen in time, free from the noises of the city. Something very raw and real remained at that little township we called home.

Many nights, A-Gong sat at his slanted drafting desk in the living room. The room would be completely dark, save for the skirt of light on a single incandescent lamp. He was always drawing something or building something. When he noticed me looking, he invited me to watch him work. I propped myself on a wooden stool next to him, close enough to pick up a faint odor of sweat and sawdust. He aligned his fountain pen to a steel ruler under the light, its luminous halo and the shadows extending from his thick calloused fingers warped with each decisive stroke. He was like a conductor when he drew. In the silence of the room, the smooth zips from his pen tip took turns with the symphony of frogs and cicadas outside. The arch on his right rear shoulder moved up and down.

A-Gong didn't grow up with a lot, so he wanted to give us everything. He hand-sawed every wooden tile in the flooring of our house and polished every inflection on the walls. He put together everything from desks and closets to child-size cars and rocking chairs for us to play with. He spent years building, plowing, and tilling the backyard to make a mini farm and grow fresh fruits and vegetables for us to eat. At the height of summer, papayas grew so full and sweet, they snapped the branches and fell to our feet. Sweet potatoes' cordate leaves poked through the soil, and heads of green cabbage bloomed like roses. Meals took place at the round table he built and consisted mostly of what he grew, simply cooked and seasoned to accentuate their natural flavors.

Ten-year-old me wouldn't be telling you about how great A-Gong and this all was. I was afraid of him. Often, I hated him. He coughed up dense phlegm from forty years of smoking and strode with fingers interlocked behind his back like a mob boss. He hardly ever smiled, let alone cried or uttered any affirmations of love. His expectations of everyone in the household were so high and insurmountable that you were better off keeping quiet around him, lest you say something that made him frown.

I would, instead, be telling you about the times we shared at the dining table. He didn't bring his sternness there. He was too busy gnawing on pork ribs, vacuuming rice with pendulum-like chopstick swipes, and taking sips of broth. He was particular about the way each dish should look and taste. He would throw a tantrum if the fish he liked to eat wasn't the correct size; but if it were, he became so chirpy, you could talk him into agreeing with pretty much anything. He spoke endlessly about which street vendor sold the best sugar-fried chestnuts and the nuances in a bowl of sesame oil chicken soup. Listening to him made me want to experience everything as he did, to imprint his flavors on my palate completely. I studied his gesture as he dusted sweet potato fries so liberally in plum powder that they almost turned pink. I added hefty dashes of white pepper the same way he did to rice noodle soup. Steam carried the pepper into our nostrils and made us sneeze. We laughed until our eyes watered and slurped the noodles like it was our first.

I was seventeen when A-Gong died. It was raining outside that morning. Or maybe it wasn't. Something else diluted the colors of the spring breeze. He lay on a bed in the middle of the living room under a white blanket. A group of Buddhist

nuns in gray robes circled him, each with their eyes closed and palms clasped. They hummed the Buddha's mantra to the tempo of a handbell. The body's separation from the soul takes eight hours, they said. It is an enormously painful process, like a thousand needles. They chanted to soothe his pain. I observed as strands of smoke from their incense sticks strung together above us into one threadbare gauze. It grew larger and larger, rose higher and higher, then disappeared. Don't cry near him, they said, for he can still hear us.

That night, the kitchen was noticeably quieter. The clatter of pots and ladles was no more. Our family had dinner at the round table and saved his seat, the one under the window. We sat and ate together and there was no conversation, no sound but the tinkling of cutlery. My chest suddenly sank into a kind of emptiness. I wondered if dinner was ever going to feel normal again. I wondered if a new normal would mean we forgot about A-Gong. Were those once familiar feelings, smells, and tastes about to dim as our memories do?

My parents and I started going to the monastery where the nuns lived, Taipei's Dizang Temple. I had no idea what to expect there. I wasn't Buddhist myself, neither was A-Gong, nor was my family. To us, Buddhism likens to the rhythms of the Earth. We don't necessarily subscribe to it or notice it. It's always there, steeped into the background noises, occasionally surfacing to give us the guidance we need. We met Huìshàn shifu, a senior nun, at the monastery. We followed her in single file through an aisle that led from the front prayer room to the back kitchen. The aisle is long and narrow enough

that you couldn't see the other end, where it led to. Turning her head slightly, shifu told us that the soul of the deceased stayed around for forty-nine days. It is at least for that time we, the immediate family, practice Buddhist precepts and accumulate gongdé (功德), "virtue from kindness." The most important part was to refuse meat. Consuming meat meant consciously harming innocent lives, and doing so set back the chances of a good re-incarnation for A-Gong.

Unlike the entrance, a red arch that enshrined golden Buddhist swastikas, the only roof over the back kitchen is a corrugated iron sheet. The nuns cooked for us there, all forty-nine days. I remember the first vegetarian bento box they made. I remember its warmth in my cold palm when I rolled off the rubber band. In the largest section of the box, a heap each of fried tofu skin rolls and lion's mane mushrooms squished together over a bed of steamed rice. The smaller dividers were filled with stir-fried greens, steamed kabocha, and roasted nuts. I balanced a mushroom floret between my chopsticks and took a small bite. Juices weeped from it.

The nuns had their way of making elegant yet unpretentious food that people might enjoy even in grieving and ascetic training. They made us sushi rolls that were as long and heavy as burritos, stuffed with vegetarian meat floss and vegetarian ham, minced bean curd, and strips of crunchy burdock root, cucumbers, and carrots. Aged mustard greens stir-fried with wheels of fried gluten that fronted a most natural musk. Savory soups stewed with medicinal herbs and all kinds of beans, seeds, and fungi. You could taste the care in each dish and each component. They grew the vegetables themselves and made the soy milk, tofu, and vegetarian meat products by hand. My dad, who usually appreciated a heavy plate of steak, took lion bites of the sushi burritos and confessed, "We should eat like this more often."

At sundown, the nuns brought food offerings to our home altar. They were meals for our departed A-Gong, and most were vegetarian meats. There

were konjak mock shrimps in colorful cups lined with romaine lettuce. They had pinkish-orange stripes just like the real thing; the transparent muscular tails looked like they could jump off the altar table when we weren't looking. Vegetarian versions of fried Taiwanese sausages, salty fish roe, and smoked shark steaks—all A-Gong's favorites— were sliced on a diagonal, neatly arranged on a plate, and garnished with purple orchids. Out of curiosity, I asked one of the nuns why they went out of their way to make and use these imitations. "It's simple." Her cheeks dimpled. "It's so that people who aren't used to eating vegetarian food can ease into the process!" I chuckled, thinking about how A-Gong would furrow his brows after trying a bite, finding out he'd been scammed. The first obstacle of afterlife is an eternally storming desert, said the nun. But the light from our positivity and prayers is powerful enough to cut through the winds and lead him down the right path.

We abstained from eating meat for a hundred days in total, or some more. The end of funeral traditions meant that Buddhist customs no longer required us to stay vegetarian. I ate my last vegetarian bento sitting on a bench outside of the crematory, and we escorted the ashes in an urn to the columbarium. I slowly introduced meat back into my diet, as did my parents. By that time, I had already lost the appetite for chunks of meat that required a fork and a knife. I frequented vegetarian restaurants because they offered the variety of vegetables and legumes I had grown accustomed to. I didn't think of it consciously then, but my outlook on food had changed.

The summer after A-Gong passed, I traveled by myself to Paris to attend Le Cordon Bleu, a survey of the fundamentals of French cooking. I practiced all the basic cuts, from the julienne to the mirepoix. I learned how to cook an egg eight different ways, how to make a tournée cut on a potato into little footballs, and how to whip up a fresh batch of mayonnaise from egg yolks and oil while managing four burners at once. I also learned how to gut and break down an entire chicken and fillet a whole fish. My passion for food began to solidify, but at the same time the gore from preparing meats made me vaguely uncomfortable. I began to think about what the nuns stood for—could I still pursue a future in food without inflicting harm to my morality and the world? And though I couldn't have fully articulated it at that time, there was also an inkling of doubt I had in my own ability to restore the home-cooking dishes that felt so imminently distant. That was why I turned to Western cooking at first. It was easier to tread into a world of foreign grandeur than dig through torn recipe pages in a ravaged home.

The following fall, I moved to California to attend college. The pandemic raged before I could finish my first year, and I relocated to live with my brother. While staying at home in lockdown, I created a food blog. It started off as a photo log of my everyday cooking, which was often just a shallow echo of what I learned at culinary school, and often still involved cooking meats. When we ran out of meat, I'd omit them from my dishes and make plant-based ones instead. I wish the vegetarian transition was a little more romantic, but really, it was just that over time and isolation, I became used to not eating meat.

Another year went by before I moved back to Taipei, where I would spend the next two years writing this book. One rainy December morning, I brought newspaper to the home altar and lit an incense stick for A-Gong. I thought again about the nuns. I phoned Huìshàn shifu and begged for a visit to the monastery. After many absent years, it was like I never left. She didn't hesitate to tell me they were making soy milk that day, and she welcomed me to join.

We made eighty gallons of soy milk in a few hours. At noon, I sat alone on a stone ledge at the kitchen courtyard and held a hot cup in my hand. I basked in the steam; it wafted of toasted soybeans. My eyes closed involuntarily, and for a few moments I just listened. The leaves on the tree next to me ruffled in the winter wind. It had started to drizzle again.

I felt each gust push some droplets onto me and tossed some past me. Of course I knew rain; I knew it didn't cling to memories. In the cold water, the sound of the nuns' chatter slowly faded with their footsteps. I got up with a sudden resolve and ran after them. What were they giggling about?

The recipes in this book are all vegan. Strictly speaking, veganism is not a thing in Taiwan. It is largely considered a Western concept, and it has made its way to Taiwan but mostly applies to Western restaurants and settings. As in the monastery, Taiwanese plant-based diets are fueled by Buddhist values. Taiwanese vegetarians don't eat alliums—scallions (蔥), garlic (蒜), chives (韭菜), onions (蕥), and asafetida (興渠)—because they unsettle the mind and the focus required for ascetic training. I keep this in mind, both in hopes to accurately render what vegetarian food is like in Taiwan and honor what the nuns have taught me. I use the alliums still when I feel it is necessary. The fragrant vegetables, after all, enrich vegetarian cooking for those not bound by Buddhist religion.

Today, I write my recipes and stories online as Chez Jorge, a name with the French preposition *chez*, meaning "at the home of." It's a word that takes me back to Paris, one that many restaurants have on their store signs to make guests feel as if they're invited into someone else's home. I pray that the fragments I've gathered here will suffice to bring about those feelings, or some new ones of your own. I'm twenty-two years old, and I don't have anything to say yet. The best I can do is to try to recollect what I can, to tell things as they are.

A Note About Language

Language and food are inexplicably linked. The fluidity of their relationship is reflected in history. Many recipes in this book will have more than one name, and I include their Taiwanese and Mandarin Chinese translations whenever applicable. Translations in Taiwanese in the text are italicized. Taiwanese (台語), also known as Holo, is a dialect evolved from the Hokkien language that some of the earliest Han Chinese (Minnan) immigrants brought with them. It traveled through the tongues of immigrants and leaderships, new and old, and so became transfused with the essences of Dutch, Hakka, Japanese, and aboriginal languages to form what it is today—a distinctly Taiwanese expression, vivid and full of emotion and imagery. People in Taiwan used to speak Taiwanese everywhere, but with the postwar takeover of 1949, the new Chinese government enforced Mandarin Chinese as Taiwan's official language (國語). Schools have stopped teaching Taiwanese since then. The only real way to learn now is through conversation, and A-Gong knew this, so he would ask me to recite the numbers and alphabets whenever he got a chance. When I walk through the traditional markets and the endearing tones of Holo surround me from all directions, I think about A-Gong and those times we'd share a car ride and he'd get me to count from one, two, and three all the way until we arrived at our destination. There's some regret, to be sure, that I didn't take his Holo lessons to heart, not grasping their importance until now. But there's also hope, knowing that through food, I can begin to understand the road A-Gong had so thoughtfully laid for me.

neutral oil   rice cooking wine   rice cooking wine
                                           (19.5% ABV)   (34% ABV)

white soy sauce   black bean white   light soy sauce   soy sauce paste   dark soy sauce
                        soy sauce

The Larder

Taiwanese people in general value health and longevity a lot. We are known for having a strong preference for qīngdàn (light-tasting food), and this is especially true for vegetarian cooking. Dishes are rarely too heavily seasoned or sauced, and instead, savored for the simplest preparations and seasonings. This doesn't mean everything is inherently bland. Condiments are just the wheels to the vehicle of ingredients, rather than the other way around. Seasonings are used just enough to bring out yuánwèi (the original flavor of the ingredients) in a way that achieves balance, engages the senses, and confirms the depth of fresh food and local produce.

The following is a list of ingredients common to the Taiwanese kitchen, what comprises them, and the contexts in which they are used. You don't need a lot to make Taiwanese dishes; most of the same ingredients and condiments apply to vegetarian and nonvegetarian food (except for some allium-free condiments, which Buddhists will use, but they don't affect the overall flavor). In this chapter, you'll also learn how to make certain staples at home, many of which you will likely not find outside of Taiwan. Everything else these recipes need should be sold at your local Asian market, 99 Ranch in particular; look online, in Taiwanese specialty shops such as Yun Hai, if there's anything you can't find.

black vinegar   rice vinegar   black vinegar
(Wu Yin)   (Tongyang)

sesame oil   toasted black   salt   white pepper
              sesame oil

Condiments

The following list of condiments is grouped by type, from the most used to least used.

Yóu 油 (neutral oil): In our home, neutral oil means sunflower oil, which has a flavor that feels most agreeable to our cooking. You can also use grapeseed oil, soybean oil, or peanut oil. Many recipes in this book utilize deep-frying, as when done right, it's a technique that can truly elevate vegetarian cooking. The key thing to know: food needs to exit the oil at a higher temperature than when you put it in; that way, excess oil escapes from the food, preventing it from soaking in grease. As long as you don't burn the oil (meaning it doesn't turn dark brown), you can use it multiple times. I keep it in a stainless-steel oil container and scoop from it whenever I cook.

Yán 鹽 (salt): When I call for salt in this book, I mean fine sea salt unless otherwise specified. You can use any salt you'd like, but you may need to adjust the volumes due to grain size. For example, ½ teaspoon of coarse salt is less salt than ½ teaspoon of fine salt.

Èrshātáng 二砂糖 (golden granulated sugar): Taiwanese home cooks rarely use white refined cane sugar for everyday cooking because it lacks nutrition and doesn't contribute much flavor. Instead, we use a semi-coarse golden sugar called èrshātáng, also called raw sugar, which is a minimally processed cane sugar that has an aroma and depth that are most natural to sugarcanes. We use this sugar not just in desserts but also in all kinds of savory applications. A small pinch is typical in stir-fries and soups to accentuate flavors without excess salt. Appropriate and timely additions of èrshātáng are key to balancing the taste of fermented foods, such as the salty *tshài-póo* (Preserved Radish, page 42) and sour suāncài (Fermented Mustard Greens, page 35). As my A-Má would say, the last thing you want is a dish that's *sí-kiâm* (死鹹), meaning "so salty it may as well have been inedible." Sugar is your remedy to that.

Bīngtáng 冰糖 (rock sugar): Crystallized rock sugar is another kind of sugar you'll see a lot in this book. It has a milder, rounder, more refreshing sweetness than cane sugar and comes in different colors—most commonly white and yellow. The white one has a pure, floral flavor that is good for cold dishes and sweet soups; the yellow one, with its more robust caramel notes, is better for braising. Since rock sugar usually comes in large clumps, I use a food processor to blend it into fine shards so it can dissolve easier in cold liquids.

Báihújiāo 白胡椒 (white pepper): The herbaceous kick of white pepper mixed with the fragrance of yóucōng (Fried Shallots, page 175) makes a flavor that is unmistakably Taiwanese to me. The ubiquitous use of white pepper in Taiwanese cuisine harkens to a time in the past, when medicinal herbs were more challenging to obtain, and people took to pepper both as a seasoning and a health food. It is believed to treat cold symptoms and aid digestion. We always have a white pepper shaker on our dining table. A hefty amount is necessary for any rice noodle dish or clear soup. I always like to add a good pinch to finish my dishes, because it wakes up the flavor. But it can also make food taste a little saltier, so note that when you're seasoning. We don't add black pepper (hēihújiāo 黑胡椒) as freely as white pepper in our cooking, though I will say, it works excellently as a source of fragrance in allium-free vegetarian dishes, and the best hújiāoyán (Pepper Salt, page 113) formulas won't do without it.

Yìnyóu 蔭油 or jiàngyóu 醬油 (light soy sauce): Next to salt, soy sauce is the most important (and frankly, the only other) salty condiment in our arsenal. We pour soy sauce liberally in our pots to flavor almost every braise, and we drizzle it in our woks to perfume many stir-fries. The original Taiwanese soy sauce is made from the black soybean, which was the only locally grown soybean before Japanese colonists brought yellow soybeans to the island. Black soybeans make a light soy sauce called yìnyóu, while yellow soybeans make one called jiàngyóu. The two are similarly savory, salty condiments—and can be used interchangeably—but they differ slightly in fragrance and depth. Yìnyóu undergoes a longer fermentation process, so it naturally has a deeper, funkier flavor than jiàngyóu. While no occasion is reserved for using either one, some will say, and justifiably, that yìnyóu gets you closer to old-time tastes. I tend to use jiàngyóu because my mom has always used jiàngyóu. It gets my food closest to the taste of hers. As a rule, when it comes to soy sauce, price generally indicates quality. Look for Taiwanese brands that are naturally brewed, rather than chemically fermented. Brands like Wanjiaxiang and Kimlan are preferable, though Kikkoman is a good approximation. Salinity may differ greatly between makes and brands (in particular, Taiwanese soy sauces are generally less salty), so it is always wise to taste before you add the full amount called for in this book's recipes.

Báijiàngyóu 白醬油 **or báiyìnyóu** 白蔭油 (**white soy sauce**): When I want to keep the original color of a dish, I reach for white soy sauce. White soy sauce has a higher wheat-to-bean ratio than light soy sauce, which makes for not only a golden amber color but also a distinctly sweeter and more delicate savory flavor. There are two types: one made with yellow soybeans (báijiàngyóu) and one made with black soybeans (báiyìnyóu). The bottle that old Taiwanese chefs will reach for is a báijiàngyóu called wèiyuányì (味原液), with Ghost Goddess brand (鬼女神) being the most iconic; but you are likely not to find it outside of Taiwan, so use Japanese brands.

Tiáohéyì 調和液 **or lǎochōu** 老抽 (**dark soy sauce**): Similar to Chinese soy sauces, Taiwanese soy sauces bear a distinction between light and dark. Light soy sauce is the one used as the main flavoring, while dark soy sauce is less salty and used for its shiny, deep molasses color.

Jiàngyóugāo 醬油膏 **or yìnyóugāo** 蔭油膏 (**soy sauce paste**): Jiàngyóugāo is a starch-thickened version of light soy sauce that is made for dipping. It's sweeter and has a coating consistency, so it doesn't soak into food the way regular soy sauce does. Yìnyóugāo is the black soybean counterpart. You can make your own soy sauce paste by thickening soy sauce with starch, as in the *uánn-kué* (Bowl Rice Cake, page 111) recipe.

Mǐjiǔ 米酒 (**rice cooking wine**): Mǐjiǔ or "michiu," as it sometimes appears on the labels of exported bottles, has an indispensable Taiwanese flavor. Today's most recognized bottle, the Red Label rice cooking wine (紅標米酒), has been produced since the 1930s, utilizing a local japonica rice cultivar called pénglái mǐ. The versatility of mǐjiǔ explains why it is so widely used in cooking. It has a mellow and clean flavor that amplifies and refines the natural taste of ingredients. Its use in the Taiwanese kitchen is endless; nearly every dish is incomplete without a small drizzle. A splash keeps homemade ferments going for months, even years. In some soups and hot pot dishes, like jiāngmǔguō (Herbal Ginger Hot Pot, page 209), mǐjiǔ replaces part or all of the water: as the alcohol boils off, it renders the broth mildly sweet, fragrant, and complex. If you can, try to source two kinds: one that is 19.5 percent ABV (alcohol by volume) for everyday cooking and one that is 34 percent ABV for infusing herbs. For those bound from imbibing by religion or other reasons, as are many Taiwanese vegetarians, use gāotāng (All-Purpose Stock, page 150) to substitute.

Xiāngyóu 香油 (sesame oil): Xiāngyóu, meaning "fragrant oil," is a light-colored sesame oil blended between the oil extracted from sesame seeds and (typically) soybeans. It has a pleasant, refreshing, nutty aroma that functions much like olive oil, but it's used more sparingly: in cold-tossed salads and dipping sauces, and as a finishing touch in hot dishes, drizzled during the final moments of cooking to reintroduce shine and freshness. You can find a bottle online or make your own by mixing one part pure toasted sesame oil with one part neutral oil.

Máyóu 麻油 or **hēimáyóu** 黑麻油 (toasted sesame oil): Máyóu is much darker in color than sesame oil (xiāngyóu), as it is made purely from toasted white sesame seeds or black sesame seeds. Toasted black sesame oil (hēimáyóu) is more typical in Taiwanese kitchens, although the toasted sesame oil you find in a Korean supermarket is a good substitute. It has a rich, powerful sesame flavor and warming effect that goes hand in hand with ginger and rice wine, making it a necessary addition in dishes such as sānbēi hóutóugū (Three Cup Lion's Mane Mushrooms, page 195).

Báicù 白醋 (rice vinegar): A clear rice vinegar, literally "white vinegar," is the most basic condiment we use to add a sharp acidity to dishes, notably quick-pickled vegetables and side dishes. When the vinegar is balanced with sugar, you get something with a pleasant cooling effect that cuts through rich, oily dishes and fried food. Japanese rice vinegar is a good substitute.

Wūcù 烏醋 (black vinegar): Like rice vinegar, wūcù is made from whole, steamed grains of sticky rice, but additional processes render its color darker and flavor much more complex. Taiwanese black vinegars are generally sweeter than other East Asian counterparts. There are no exact substitutions; you'll need a bottle if you want to re-create the distinct Taiwanese flavors. Different brands conjure different flavors, and the recipes in this book will specify which one is preferred, but you can use them interchangeably. There are three different types they typically fall under: fruit and vegetable infused (such as Kong Yen), spice and herb infused (such as Tongyang), and naturally aged (such as Wu Yin).

Wèisù 味素 (monosodium glutamate): Also known most commonly as MSG, "the essence of taste" is a seasoning composed of salt and a glutamate that gives it an umami taste. The latter, although isolated in a lab, is chemically identical to the same naturally occurring stuff that gives tomatoes and mushrooms their savory flavors. Taiwanese vegetarian cooks, particularly the Buddhist nuns, use MSG (and bouillon powders) prolifically because they cannot use most aromatics. Using MSG at home is largely your own choice, but know that less is more. You don't want to add MSG excessively or to every dish, because it would make them all taste the same. When you see recipes calling for the optional addition of MSG in this book, the recipes generally contain a significant proportion of (1) spice, (2) medicinal herbs, or (3) preserved food. These are ingredients that contain naturally bitter or acrid tastes, which can be accentuated since we aren't using meat to supply the balance that is usually in place. Adding small amounts of MSG in these cases helps round out those flavors, should you find them unpalatable.

香菇粉 xiānggūfěn | hiunn-koo-hún

Mushroom Powder

This is essentially ground-up gānxiānggū (dried shiitake mushrooms, see page 24). You can find store-bought versions, but they may add some chemical fragrances. This recipe has less umami than store-bought counterparts, but it tastes and smells natural. We experience umami much more when different umami compounds combine, hence the mix of mushrooms and kombu.

Makes about ⅓ cup (80g)

25 medium dried shiitake mushrooms (65g)

6 (3-inch) pieces kombu (15g)

½ tsp (2g) white rock sugar

½ tsp (3g) salt

1 Preheat the oven to 175°F (80°C), with convection on if available.

2 Break or snip the shiitake mushrooms and kombu into ½-inch chunks. Spread the mushrooms and kombu in a single layer on a baking tray and dehydrate in the oven for 1 to 3 hours; this will depend on how stale your mushrooms and kombu are. When fully dehydrated, the mushroom pieces should snap with some resistance like fine dark chocolate, and the kombu should snap like crackers. If they don't, continue to dehydrate until they do.

3 Remove the tray from the oven and let all the pieces cool to room temperature. Grind the mushroom, kombu, rock sugar, and salt together in a spice or coffee grinder until very, very fine, so fine that you feel an umami tingle in your nostrils as you lift the lid of the grinder.

4 Transfer the powder through a fine sieve to an airtight glass container. You can blend the bits collected in the sieve to get more powder out of them. Store in a cool, dry place (or in the refrigerator if it's humid) for up to 6 months.

辣椒醬 làjiāojiàng

Fermented Chili Paste

Fermenting takes away the grassy taste that comes with raw chilies and supplants it with a fruity and complex flavor. Adding a fruit like apple or pineapple makes this chili paste sweet, floral, and bright, something you won't find in many commercial chili pastes. Use the red chilies available to you locally; in Taiwan, I use a mix of mild and hot varieties of red cháotiānjiāo (朝天椒, heaven-facing chili). Blooming this in equal parts oil can wake up its flavor for a dipping sauce.

Makes 2 cups

10½ oz (300g) fresh red chilies

Salt

1 Tbsp golden granulated sugar

1 Tbsp Taiwanese rice cooking wine, plus more for rinsing

⅛ apple (30g), peeled and roughly chopped

1 Rinse the chilies and pat them dry. Set aside to air-dry for 1 to 2 hours, until completely dry.

2 Trim and discard the chilies' tops and remove some of the seeds. I tend to remove the seeds from all but six to eight of the milder red chilies. When the chilies are prepared, weigh them and multiply that number by 5 percent—this is the weight of salt you need.

3 Add the salt, sugar, rice cooking wine, and apple to the bowl of a food processor. Process until mostly smooth, then add the chilies. Pulse a few more times to chop the chilies into a rough paste with visible flakes.

4 Rinse a lidded 2-cup jar with about 1 Tbsp rice cooking wine and pour it out. Pack the chili paste into the container. Press down as you pack to push out all the air bubbles. Cover the surface of the paste with a layer of plastic wrap to mitigate direct air contact (otherwise it is susceptible to yeast growth; see page 31). Secure the lid.

5 Let ferment at room temperature for 15 to 20 days. As it ferments, the raw, grassy smell of the chilies will mellow, and a deep fruity aroma will take its place. Once the flavor and aroma are at your desired depth, move the jar to the refrigerator to slow the ferment and store for up to 1 year.

甜辣醬 tiánlàjiàng
Sweet Chili Sauce

Every family has their few go-to tabletop chili sauces. Sweet chili sauce is one that's always on our dining table, usually in the narrow glass jar that has "the flavor of love (愛之味)" on its label. This is my replica, a sweet and not-very-spicy red sauce that coats food in the same satisfying way. You can substitute the store-bought version.

1 In a small saucepan, combine the sugar, ketchup, mushroom powder, fermented chili paste, and ½ cup of the water. Bring to a boil, then lower the heat to a simmer and cook for 1 minute to mellow the acidity of the ketchup and infuse all the flavors.

2 Meanwhile, make a slurry by whisking the glutinous rice flour with the remaining ¼ cup water. Drizzle the slurry into the simmering sauce while whisking constantly to incorporate. Bring to a boil again to thicken the sauce. Remove from the heat and set aside to cool.

3 Pour the cooled sauce into an airtight glass container and refrigerate for up to 2 months.

Makes about 1 cup

¼ cup (50g) golden granulated sugar

¼ cup (65g) ketchup

½ tsp Mushroom Powder 香菇粉 (page 15) or use store-bought

2 Tbsp Fermented Chili Paste 辣椒醬 (page 16) or use store-bought

¾ cup water

2 tsp glutinous rice flour 糯米粉

糖蒜 tángsuàn

Pickled Garlic

Pickling mellows a lot of garlic's inherent spicy acridness and infuses it with the sweet, malty, molasses-y flavor of the black vinegar brine. Eat this as a side dish or use it as a condiment to bring a depth of flavor to some of the simplest vegetable preparations, such as the dìguāyè (Blanched Sweet Potato Leaves, page 135). The longer the garlic ages, the deeper and more rounded the flavor.

Makes one 4-cup jar

2 cups water

4 tsp (24g) salt

14 oz (400g) unpeeled garlic cloves

1 cup rice vinegar 白醋

¼ cup Taiwanese black vinegar 烏醋

1 cup (210g) dark brown sugar 黑糖

1 In a bowl, combine the water and salt and stir until fully dissolved. Add the garlic cloves to the salt water and soak overnight.

2 The next day, drain the salt water. Pat the garlic cloves dry and let them sit in a bamboo drying basket or steel tray under the sun for 1 hour, until dry to the touch. If there happens to be no sun in the foreseeable days or weeks, you can also let them air-dry for 3 to 4 hours in a cool place.

3 Meanwhile, in a saucepan, combine the rice vinegar, black vinegar, and dark brown sugar. Bring to a boil over high heat and then reduce to a simmer. Stir to dissolve the sugar, about 30 seconds. Set aside to cool.

4 Pack the garlic cloves into a lidded 4-cup glass container. Follow with the completely cooled vinegar brine; it should just be enough to cover all the garlic cloves; make more brine according to the ratio if necessary. Place a sanitized rock or a small dish on top of the garlic to keep them submerged in the brine. Secure the lid and let ferment at room temperature out of direct sunlight for at least 1 month. The pickled garlic can be stored in an airtight container for up to 2 years; keep in the refrigerator after opening.

Dry Goods

To keep recipes accessible, I use a lot of dry goods. Most of the ingredients called for can be found in any grocery store. For some specific Asian products, visit a local Asian grocery store or search online. Here are some to note.

Gānxiānggū 乾香菇 (dried shiitake mushrooms): Dried shiitake mushrooms perfume many Taiwanese dishes, vegetarian or not. Lots of recipes start with *khiàn-phang* (爆香), which means frying or "exploding" the fragrance of aromatics in oil, and you'll often see dried shiitake mushrooms follow the aromatic vegetables. The mushrooms' drying process produces lots of umami compounds (primarily guanylic acid) and creates a distinctly firm, meaty texture. Use room temperature or warm water to rehydrate them, and this can take 10 minutes or up to 3 hours depending on your mushrooms. Hot water is always faster, but know that you'll get only a fraction of the flavor in comparison. Look for mushrooms that are strongly fragrant (high quality), crisp (not stale), and aren't too thick (rehydrate faster). Japanese brands tend to more closely resemble the Taiwanese stuff.

Kūnbù 昆布 (kombu): The first MSG was isolated from the glutamic acid found in kombu, so you bet they are packed to the brim with umami! I use kombu in my gāotāng (All-Purpose Stock, page 150), which acts as a base for many of my recipes. The type and make of kombu will affect a broth's taste and color, but for home-cooking purposes, I wouldn't dwell too much on the specifics. Just use one that is affordable and accessible. For clearer broths, look for Ma-kombu (真昆布) or Rishiri-kombu (利尻昆布). Don't rinse the kombu; simply wipe it with a paper towel if there is any visible dust (the white powder is perfectly normal and a source of umami).

Beans and legumes: The recipes in this book use fresh or dried—never canned—beans and legumes, as is typical of Taiwanese kitchens.

Nuts and seeds: For cooking, buy unroasted, unsalted nuts and seeds. Toast them in a hot pan or in a 355°F (180°C) oven for a few minutes to unleash their maximum flavors. Freshly roasted nuts are great for making pastes, such as white or black sesame pastes or peanut butter; process them in a food processor until their natural oils are released—you won't need to add a drop of oil. Pre-roasted nuts have their place, too, but more for direct eating. The Buddhist nuns often add a handful of mixed nuts or sunflower seeds to improve the nutritional content of their meals.

Flours and starches: For all-purpose flour, use Asian brands, typically ones with steamed buns on the packaging. Sunright brand (日正) is preferable. Compared to American brands, they make softer and more refined doughs. Don't treat dough and water ratios as exacts; absorption can differ due to many factors, so it's best to leave a 1 tablespoon water buffer. For thickening sauces, potato starch is most common to what's used in Taiwanese kitchens, but cornstarch is just fine. You'll need a coarse sweet potato starch to dust fried food, for that signature Taiwanese bubbly crackling crust, and a fine sweet potato starch for general applications like thickening soups and supplying a springy texture to flour crepes and rice cakes.

Spices

Stock up on whole spices and the recipes in this book will be at your fingertips. Following are two essential spice blends, Five-Spice and Thirteen-Spice, both of which can be either ground to powder or added as whole spices to recipes. Every cook and every brand in Taiwan will make these blends a little differently. Experiment and feel free to add something new, a little more of one spice, or a little less of another, to get a flavor profile that you like. You can also find the spice blends sold at Asian markets, to save some time; for powders, I recommend Tomax brand (小磨坊) five-spice and Wang Shou Yi (王守義) brand thirteen-spice.

To make a powder: Add all the spices to a dry skillet and set it over medium heat. Toast for 2 to 3 minutes, or until fragrant and popping. Set aside to cool, then grind them finely in a spice or coffee grinder. If there are any large or still unground bits, strain out the powder and grind the coarse bits once or twice more. Keep in an airtight glass jar, preferably in the refrigerator, and use within 6 months.

To make a braising pouch (for ease of removal after the flavors are infused): Nestle all the whole spices into a braising sachet or wrap them with a piece of cheesecloth. Use two sachets if the spices won't fit into one. Tie a knot to secure the braising pouch(es).

五香 **wǔxiāng**

Five-Spice

Like in China, in Taiwan we prolifically use a spice blend called "five spice." It was first brought over from China but has evolved since, in large part to conform to local tastes. The tingly heat of Sichuan peppercorns, in particular, is much more muted in Taiwanese-style formulas—the Taiwanese aren't good with food that is too numbing. The sweet spicy warmth of cinnamon takes its place.

6 whole star anise pods (10g)

2 Tbsp (8g) red Sichuan peppercorns

1 (6-inch) cinnamon stick (12g), snapped into pieces

4 tsp (10g) fennel seeds

3 tsp (5g) coriander seeds

30 whole cloves (3g)

十三香 **shísānxiāng**

Thirteen-Spice

This is my secret weapon to bring food, especially braised stuff such as lǔwèi (Soy-Braised Goods, page 116), from "that's good" to "wow." It's an extension of five-spice that adds an array of subtle flavors for balance and complexity. In carefully crafted proportions, no single spice punches out at you: you get something that I'd describe as qīngxiāng (清香), a coyly sweet flavor and elegant scent that you can't quite get tired of.

9 whole star anise pods (12g)

1½ Tbsp (8g) red Sichuan peppercorns

3 Tbsp (12g) gui zhi (cinnamon twigs)

1 (1-inch) cinnamon stick (2g)

4 tsp (10g) fennel seeds

20 whole cloves (2g)

2 Tbsp (16g) shan nai (sand ginger)

4 slices bai zhi (dahurian angelica) (8g)

2 tsp (3g) chen pi (dried black tangerine peel)

4 sha ren (amomum pods) (2g)

5 whole dried bay leaves (1g)

9 white cardamom pods (2g)

1 whole tsaoko (Chinese black cardamom) (3g), smacked open

Equipment

Saying you need any highly specific or obscure tools is a ridiculous affront to the way we cook for A-Gong's table. Don't let anyone tell you that empty rice wine bottles won't make excellent rolling pins, or an old cotton T-shirt can't be used for straining soy milk. There are some tools that will make your life in the kitchen a lot easier, but don't let their absence stop you if you have the urge to make something. The most important part of home cooking is to make use of what you have and what feels comfortable for you.

A rice cooker (diànguō 電鍋) is the only tool for which I will tell you to drop this book right now and run to the store. My mom dubs it "the most amazing-est invention in the world." Tatung (大同) is the brand we use, and we have it in all different shapes and sizes. (If you're looking to get only one, get the 6-cup one.) Their products are so solid, we've been using the same ones for twenty years. We use a rice cooker not just for cooking rice, but for any recipe that needs an even, gentle, and indirect heat, such as lǜdòu yìrén (Mung Bean Soup with Pearl Barley, page 119) or the stewed peanuts in dòuhuā (Tofu Pudding with Stewed Peanuts and Sweet Red Beans, page 121).

Aside from that, of course, you'll need some basic tools, such as a chef's knife, cutting board, mixing bowls, slotted spoons and strainers, different sizes of pots and pans, lidded jars in various sizes (1-cup, 2-cup, 3-cup, and 4-cup), plus a few of the niftier gadgets like a vegetable peeler and a tofu cloth or cheesecloth. A digital scale and a thermometer will come in handy if you'd like to be precise. A nice knife is your best investment, and I love my càidāo (菜刀, vegetable cleaver) because it has a wide and hefty yet thin blade that can be used not just for delicate cuts but also for smacking and pounding. If you have one, get yourself a wooden chopping board (I like those that look like oversize hockey pucks), as it's less harsh on the knife's edge. Sharpen the knife often.

For stir-frying, I have two round-bottomed carbon steel woks, one 13-inch (makes portions for two to four) and one 14-inch (makes portions for four to six). Both are totally black from the patina built after years of stir-frying. A screaming-hot wok set over fire gives food a smoky, complex flavor that makes it taste more alive. The wok also lasts a lifetime as long as you use it often and keep it dry. But for all purposes, a Teflon nonstick pan works just fine on any regular gas or induction stove. I tend to steam food with a bamboo steamer, which keeps the top of food dry and imparts a delicious fragrance, but for the purposes of this book, any steel steamer setup, such as placing a steel rack in a sauté pan and setting the food on top, will work. You can also steam food in your trusty rice cooker; you just need to fit an inverted bowl inside to elevate the food.

In recipes, I specify whether to use a blender or food processor. Blenders are better for blitzing wet ingredients to a smooth texture, and food processors are better at chopping dry ingredients into uniform shapes like flakes. Spice or coffee grinders are compact and effective for making powders, but a mortar and pestle or even the bottom of a pan can work, too.

I'm a sucker for old things. I keep all the old plates, bowls, and pots that A-Gong used to collect. Some bowls have been washed so many times that the original polish of the white ceramic has taken on an ivory sheen. Some clay pots have braised so much lǔròu (braised pork) that they're covered in a web of cracks and the bottom is burnt black. I keep the dishes for those indelible wears. Cooking and eating from them lets me think of him often.

Preserved
Vegetables

He said: *Now that I think about it, the dishes my mom cooked often stemmed from a kind of frugality. With the country wrought in recession, it was difficult to make ends meet. Fresh ingredients did not always come by, and we did not have meat except for special occasions. Still, each night, she filled the dining table with a colorful spread of dishes. She boiled pineapple skins to make a hot golden "tea" and salted daikon radish skins and their thick green stalks to make pickles. She braised the pork trimmings she bartered from the meat vendor with a fragrant mixture of soy sauce, rice wine, and fried shallots, and poured it over the yellowing sweet potato leaves that the vegetable vendor couldn't sell. It feels wrong to be longing for those dishes. Why do I reminisce about those less fortunate times?*

Jiàngcài, meaning "food preserved in sauce," is not only about preserving food but also about preserving a piece of Taiwanese resilience. Minnan and Hakka groups, people we know today as "Taiwanese," were all immigrants at the start. Fermentation takes us to their lives cultivating land in a new environment, where the flow of food was uncertain, either scarce or harvested in large, sporadic surpluses. Salting the food made it last longer and allowed farmers to prolong the abundant harvests and subsequently survive the not-so-abundant ones.

I remembered that the nuns hardly wasted anything in the kitchen. When a jar of sauce or condiment emptied, they took it as a vessel to add water to their dishes. Every bit clinging to the jars rinsed off. In the morning when we made soy milk, one of the nuns squatted over a stool next to the soy milk machines. She clawed her palm inside the tofu cloth for the flecks of soybean pulp stuck along the seams, collecting them to sprinkle over the soil as plant fertilizers. I told her I noticed how meticulous she and the other nuns were when it came to minimizing waste. "It's the smallest greatest thing you can do," she replied, looking at me. "It's what we call xífú (惜福), to show that you cherish the abundance and fortune that this world has given to you."

Xífú. I chewed the intonations in my mouth, making it last a little longer.

Jiàngcài Basics

Preserving food is about extending shelf life, but *don't use ingredients that are at the brink of death*. The best ferments are made using quality, fresh produce.

To achieve accurate results, treat fermentation like lab work. You need to be clean and precise. This means using hand soap before handling food and making sure all utensils are boiled (sterilized) and wiped dry—whether it be making the ferment or accessing it later. This also means using a digital scale to weigh every ingredient.

The best vessel for your ferments is an airtight jar made with nonreactive materials such as glass or clay. Always try to find suitably sized jars for your ferments, as you don't want to leave too much room for air and unwanted microbes to grow. Before you start any ferment, you need to sterilize your fermentation jars. Either use a dishwasher or place the jars in boiling water for 3 to 5 minutes, then let them stand until they are fully cooled and dry. Take this time to boil and sterilize any weights that you may use as well.

Timely uses of heavy weights create texture; don't skip it! You'll need some weight plates or rocks (10 to 15 kilograms', or 20 to 30 pounds', worth) to weigh down ingredients when water needs to be expelled. If your weights are dirty and not easily disinfected, you can wrap them in large plastic bags, such as clean trash bags, before using.

Throughout the fermenting process, monitor your ferments closely to see if any mold or yeast develops. The main tell between mold and yeast is that mold will look fuzzy and raised and is usually colorful—such as blue, green, or black. Yeast is thin, flimsy looking, and generally white. Once you see mold in a jar, the whole thing is contaminated; throw it out and start again. Yeast, on the other hand, is generally harmless but not tasty and is best removed. Scoop the yeast out using a sterilized spoon (boiled and wiped dry) and add a shallow layer of salt at the surface to prevent its regrowth.

Water: Whereas for cooking you may use tap water, for ferments it is safest to use sterilized—boiled and cooled—water.

Salt: Every technique we use to preserve food, in some way, controls the amount of water present in the ingredients. To draw out water, most recipes start with salt and a brief sunbath. For all fermentation, it is standard practice to use a coarse non-iodized salt. The coarse grind provides the abrasion necessary for the salt to penetrate the food, and the absence of iodine allows the food to maintain its original color. The seasoning for recipes in this book is calibrated to my homemade ferments. If you are using store-bought versions of these ferments, know that salinity may differ greatly. Follow the package directions, and always taste the ferments if you are not sure. You may need to soak them in water to reduce excess salt and/or preservatives.

Sugar: Because fermented foods have high concentrations of salt, sugar is there to provide balance. Use the same sugars as those used for cooking—golden granulated sugar or rock sugar, depending on the ferment.

Koji: Many Taiwanese ferments use koji, a fungus of the genus *Aspergillus* (and species *oryzae* and *sojae*). It is the same fungus that Japanese fermenters use to make miso and shoyu, those savory-sweet flavors we all know and love. You'll need two types of koji for this book: soybean and rice. Soybean koji provides the primary flavor, while rice koji gives an additional complexity and fragrance. Combined in different contexts and proportions, they yield different flavors and aromas. Find them at Japanese grocery stores or online.

Rice cooking wine: Sometimes the sanitized jars sit in the cabinet for a long time, so to be extra safe, I rinse them once more with rice cooking wine (which is usually already called for in recipes) right before bottling. To rinse, pour a small splash into the jar and tightly secure the lid. Invert and shake the jar to get all parts of the interior glass and rim. If preparing multiple jars at once, you can conserve the rice cooking wine by pouring it into the next jar and continuing for the next, until all the jars are rinsed.

Gan cao (dried licorice root): If there's one adjective to describe the flavor Taiwanese people love, it is *kam-tinn* (甘甜)—that gentle sweet aftertaste that lingers at the back of the tongue, like a sip of good tea. This ingredient is the source of that flavor. A few slices can infuse its sweetness and light herbal fragrance into the entire ferment.

Suāncài (*left*), fúcài (*middle*), méigāncài (*right*). These are all products of Swatow mustard. With different degrees of moisture and age, the mustard takes on different flavors and aromas. Méigāncài (梅乾菜) is the result of a year's worth of additional drying and aging to suāncài. Fúcài (福菜) is a half-dried product, something in between. Both are called *phak-tshài* (覆菜) in Taiwanese.

酸菜 suāncài | 鹹菜 kiâm-tshài
Fermented Mustard Greens

Every culture has their way of keeping a stinking jar of vegetables in the larder, and in Taiwan, it takes the delicious form of suāncài. Swatow mustards themselves are peppery and bitter, but after fermenting, they take on an alluring sourness and a fragrance that is difficult to resist. Look for young, vibrantly green heads of swatow mustard. Old yellowing ones have fibrous stalks that won't be very nice to eat. If you can't find swatow mustard, baby mustard and gai lan are good substitutes. Lacto-fermentation is a great way to repurpose rice-washing water, the starchy water that results from washing rice. It enriches the brine with nutrients and additional lactic acid bacteria to improve the ferment.

1   Rinse the mustards thoroughly, especially toward the inner center of the bulb, where dirt and bugs tend to gather. Pat them dry and let sit under the sun for 4 to 8 hours, until dry to the touch and slightly wrinkled. If there is no sun in the foreseeable days or weeks, you can let them air-dry for up to 24 hours in a cool place.

2   Weigh the mustard greens and multiply that number by 3 percent—that is the weight of the salt you need. Place the mustard greens in a very large bowl, sprinkle with the salt, and massage the salt onto every surface. You should start to smell the fragrance of mustard as you rub salt on the stems and leaves.

3   Once the mustard greens are moist throughout, about 5 minutes in, cover them with a plate. Weigh them down with heavy weights (about 25 lb) for 12 hours. The mustard greens will shrink significantly as some liquid seeps out.

4   To make the brine: Place the white rice in a large sieve (generally, I just use 1 to 1½ cups of rice—or however much I will cook later that day). Rinse the rice under running water for 5 seconds (to rid any dust

*Makes 2 heads
(about 1,000g total)*

2 medium heads swatow mustard 大芥菜/刈菜 (1,200g), whole (or halve them if large)

Salt, preferably a coarse non-iodized pickling salt

Taiwanese rice cooking wine, for rinsing

Brine

Short-grain white rice

2½ cups rice-washing water 洗米水, or enough to cover

Salt

(continued)

or impurities), drain, and transfer to a bowl. Add water to cover, then swirl the rice as you would if you were washing it, until the water turns a creamy, murky white. Separate the rice and water by pouring the rice into a sieve over another bowl, and reserve that starchy water. Repeat, washing until you have 2½ cups of it (though you may need more, depending on how much liquid has seeped out of the vegetables). Weigh the water and multiply that number by 3 percent; that is the weight of the salt you need to add to the brine. Store the washed rice in the refrigerator for up to 2 days if not cooking the day of.

5 Rinse an airtight lidded 4-cup glass container with about 1 Tbsp rice cooking wine and pour it out. Pack the mustard greens tightly into the container. Top with the brine (it should be enough to just cover the greens; make more brine if necessary). Secure a sterilized rock or a small cup on top of the greens to press them below the brine level. Secure the lid.

6 Ferment at room temperature and out of direct sunlight for 14 to 21 days. When it smells sufficiently sour, move the container to the refrigerator to slow the ferment. Store for up to 6 months.

Variation: Blanching Shortcut

This quicker method is convenient in cloudy and rainy places, one I especially favor after making a batch of suāncài the traditional way and having leftover brine. Start with weighing the mustards and calculating the salt needed (3 percent by weight) as in step 2 of the preceding recipe. Wash the mustards as you normally would, then plunge the heads into boiling water for 5 seconds and no longer (otherwise you risk killing off the bacteria you need for fermentation). The greens will shrink to a manageable size, so you can skip the sunbath and heavy weights. Let the greens cool and pat them dry. Proceed with making the rice-washing water brine as instructed in step 4 of the preceding recipe. Before bottling, add the old brine, if available, as a starter.

雪菜 xuěcài | 新醃咸菜 sin-kiâm-tshài

Preserved Greens

Xuěcài is basically suāncài (page 35) without letting the vegetable truly ferment and acidify so it retains its peppery sharpness. Besides baby mustard greens, bok choy, aburana (油菜), komatsuna (小松菜), and turnip leaves (蘿蔔葉) can all be made into xuěcài, and each results in its own unique texture and flavor.

1 Rinse the baby mustard greens thoroughly, especially near the root ends where dirt and bugs tend to gather. Smack or cut into the thickest parts of the stem, where salt might not easily penetrate. Pat the greens dry and let sit in the sun for 1 to 2 hours, until dry to the touch and the stems are softened. If there happens to be no sun in the foreseeable days or weeks, you can also let them air-dry for up to 6 hours in a cool place.

2 Weigh the greens and multiply that number by 2 percent—that is the weight of salt you need. Place the greens in a large bowl, sprinkle with the salt, and massage it gently onto every surface. Once all the greens are coated with salt, set them aside for 20 to 30 minutes. The leaves should take on a vibrant green color and some liquid should have seeped out.

3 Pack the greens and all their liquid into a food storage bag or an airtight lidded 2-cup glass container. Secure the bag or the lid. Let it ferment at room temperature out of direct sunlight for 1 day, then move it to the refrigerator. The flavor and fragrance will gradually deepen as you let it sit. Store in the refrigerator for up to 1 month.

Makes 8 stalks (about 300g total)

8 stalks baby mustard greens 小芥菜 (600g) or greens of choice

Salt, preferably a coarse non-iodized pickling salt

菜脯 tshài-póo

Preserved Radish

A-Gong spent the first few days of each January at the Bali District with his friends, who are master fermenters. Against the backdrop of the Tamsui River, they sat on the ground with their backs arched, using their wrinkly hands to scrub salt on pieces of daikon radish. They lined up the pieces one by one outside the porch under the winter sun. Every few hours they rotated and flipped the pieces to allow even sunlight coverage. Days elapsed, and a truckload of daikon radishes shrank into mere bags, a fraction of the original volume. Just like suāncài (Fermented Mustard Greens, page 35), *tshài-póo* is a job for winter. Cold weather is when the daikon radishes are at their sweetest, as they generate sugars to fight the frost. I liken the process of preserving radishes to crafting sourdough, as it is one that requires not a lot of active time but consecutive days of attention and care. Before you start, remember to check the weather forecast. You'll need at least 1 week of sunlight and no rain to complete this in one go!

Makes 24 pieces (about 300g total)

6 medium daikon radishes (3,000g)

Salt, preferably a coarse, non-iodized pickling salt

Taiwanese rice cooking wine, for rinsing

1 **Day 1:** Start in the morning by peeling two layers off the exterior of the daikon radishes. The daikon should look slightly transparent, not completely white. The interior skin of the daikon can be slightly bitter, so make sure you thoroughly peel it! Quarter the daikon lengthwise (you can also halve them crosswise if they are very long). Weigh the radishes and multiply that number by 6 percent—that is the total weight of the salt you need. Take note of the original weight of the peeled radishes, as it will be helpful later in monitoring the drying progress. Place the radishes in a very large bowl and sprinkle with half of the salt to start. Massage the radishes with the salt; you should feel their surfaces instantly become moist. Cover the radishes with a plate and weigh it down with heavy weights (about 25 lb) for 12 hours. After that time, a lot of water should have seeped out. Pour off that water and sprinkle on the remaining salt. Toss to coat all the radishes evenly with the salt.

(continued)

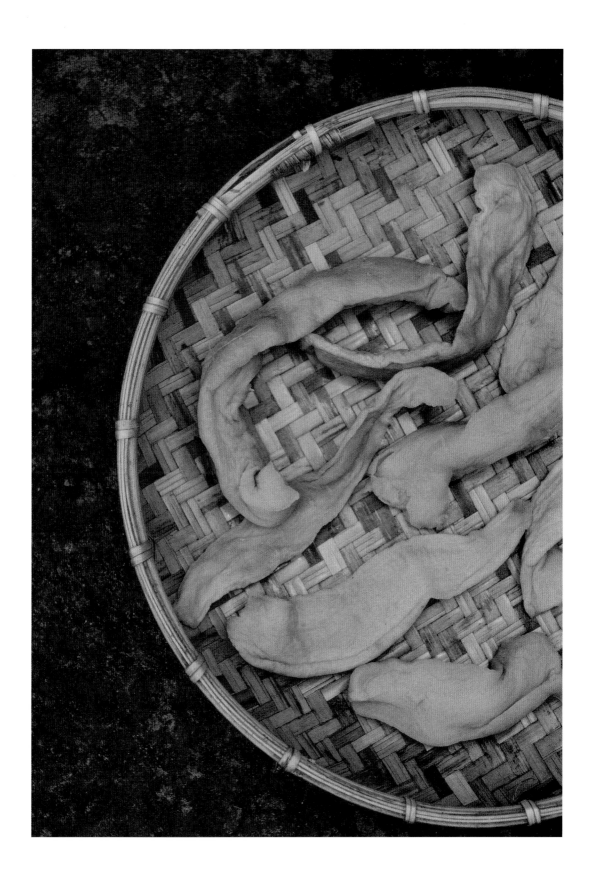

Preserved Radish —— continued

Re-cover the radishes with the plate and weights for another 12 hours, until the radishes easily bend into a U shape.

2 **Day 2:** Take the radishes out of the bowl and dry their surfaces with a paper towel. Lay them out in a single layer on a bamboo drying basket or steel tray and place them under the sun for the duration of the day. Flip them every 6 hours or so if you can (or remember to dry the other side the next day). When the sun goes down, retrieve the radishes and pack them into a sealed container. Store at room temperature.

3 **Day 3 (and counting):** Repeat the drying process until the radishes are 10 to 15 percent of their original peeled weight. This could take between 3 and 8 days more, depending on how hot the sun is. At the end of the drying process, they should be slightly squishy, not completely dried to a crisp, and brownish yellow from exposure to sunlight.

4 Rinse an airtight lidded 3-cup glass jar with about 1 Tbsp rice cooking wine and pour it out. Pack the radishes tightly into the jar. Secure the lid and refrigerate until ready to use. I generally start to use these after aging them for another 2 weeks. As the radishes sit, they will continue to darken in color and deepen in flavor. Unless mold grows, there is no expiration date.

醬冬瓜 jiàngdōngguā | 冬瓜醬 tang-kue tsiùnn

Winter Melon in Soybean Sauce

This salty-sweet ferment infuses winter melon with the gentle umami tastes of koji. A-Gong always kept a jar in the cabinet under the sink. He'd scoop from it whenever he ate congee or needed something that could provide instant flavor to a light steamed dish. It seems that A-Gong always viewed winter melons in a special way. Like sweet potatoes, the gourds grow everywhere and aren't worth a lot. "Winter" is in the name not because it's a wintertime crop, but because it can last in the larder all the way from summer harvest through the height of winter when there are fewer other fruits to eat. They're always there when you need them. So even in the dreary cold, you can still have a taste of summer. Isn't that why we ferment?

Pick a slice of winter melon that has fewer seeds in the middle—these have thicker flesh that will remain firm and tender instead of mushy when preserved. Mushiness isn't a problem, but it is a little less convenient when these are cooked in soup. The red chili is there as a background flavor and natural preservative; it won't make the ferment spicy.

Makes one 4-cup jar

1 (2-inch-thick) slice winter melon (1,000g), about 700g after peeling and seeding

Salt, preferably a coarse non-iodized pickling salt

⅓ cup (70g) soybean koji 豆麴/豆粕

2 Tbsp (30g) rice koji 米麴

⅔ cup Taiwanese rice cooking wine, or enough to cover, preferably 19.5 percent ABV, plus more for rinsing

1 Tbsp (15g) golden granulated sugar

1 small fresh red chili, seeded and chopped (optional)

4 pieces gan cao (dried licorice root) 甘草 (5g)

1 Slice off the green skin of the winter melon, then cut it into 3- to 4-inch-long chunks. Use a spoon to scrape off and discard the seeds and any spongy tissue that surrounds them.

2 Weigh the winter melon chunks and multiply that number by 7.5 percent—that is the weight of the salt you need. Place the winter melon chunks in a large bowl and toss them with the salt. Let sit for 1 hour, by which time liquid should pool in the bowl.

3 Preheat the oven to 150°F (65°C). Line a baking tray with parchment paper.

4 Pour off the liquid that has seeped out and place the winter melon chunks on the prepared baking tray. Dehydrate the chunks in the oven

(continued)

for about 2 hours, flipping halfway through, until their surfaces are dry and wrinkled and appear spongy. Remove from the oven, set aside, and let cool to room temperature.

5 Mix the soybean and rice koji in a bowl. Rinse with ¼ cup of the rice cooking wine for a few seconds to rid it of any dust or impurities. You don't want them too clean, as you'll be washing away some of the koji spores as well. Drain the koji and add it to a mixing bowl. Add the granulated rock sugar and stir together.

6 Rinse a lidded 4-cup glass container with about 1 Tbsp of the rice cooking wine and pour it out. Pack a layer of the koji mixture into the bottom of the container. Follow with a layer of the cooled winter melon chunks, leaving gaps between each chunk, then add another layer of the koji mixture, filling those gaps. If using, disperse some of the chopped red chilies in each layer. Pack the chunks in so that all sides of the winter melon touch the koji mixture. The last layer should be the koji mixture. Place the gan cao at the top and add the remaining ⅔ cup rice cooking wine (or enough to fill up the container, leaving as little room for air as possible). Secure the lid.

7 Let ferment at room temperature, out of direct sunlight, for at least 1 month and preferably 3 months. Come back to check on it once after a day or two. The winter melon tends to absorb some rice wine, so you may need to add a little more. The color of the rice wine will turn dark brown when the ferment is ready. Store for up to 2 years at room temperature; refrigerate after opening.

醬瓜 jiànggū | 醬瓜仔 tsiùnn-kue-á

Cucumbers in Sweet Soy Sauce

Apple-crisp cucumbers (page 48, left) are always part of A-Gong's jiàngcài (preserved vegetable) spreads. In the heart of every kid who grew up in Taiwan, nothing beats a good soy-preserved cucumber at livening up some congee or a bowl of rice.

1 Use a sponge to scrub off the prickly spines, if there are any, on the cucumbers. Trim both ends off each cucumber, then cut them into even ½-inch chunks.

2 Weigh the cucumbers and multiply that number by 2 percent—that is the weight of the salt you need. Place the cucumbers in a large bowl and toss them with the salt. Let sit for 10 minutes, by which time the liquid should have seeped out and pooled at the bottom of the bowl. Discard the liquid.

3 Pack the cucumbers into a tofu cloth or cheesecloth and set the cloth in a flat tray (for holding any water that is squeezed out). Twist the cloth to tightly pack the cucumber chunks. Weigh this down with heavy weights (about 10 kg or 25 lb) for 1 to 2 hours, or until the cucumbers slightly shrink, become pliable, and take on a uniform, slightly translucent dark green color.

4 To make the soy sauce brine: In a small saucepan, combine the light soy sauce, golden granulated sugar, and rice cooking wine. Bring to a boil over high heat, then reduce the heat and simmer for 1 to 2 minutes to fully dissolve the sugar and cook off the alcohol. Set aside to cool.

5 In a lidded 4-cup glass container, pack the cucumbers. Pour the cooled soy sauce brine over the cucumbers and secure the lid.

6 Refrigerate for at least 3 days before enjoying. Store in the refrigerator for up to 2 months.

Makes one 4-cup jar

6 Asian cucumbers
小黃瓜 (600g)

Salt

Soy Sauce Brine

1⅓ cups light soy sauce

1 cup (200g) golden granulated sugar

¼ cup Taiwanese rice cooking wine, preferably 19.5 percent ABV

Both of these preserves can be abbreviated as *kue-á* (瓜仔), and some people use them interchangeably, but they confer very different flavors. Jiàngguā (on the left) is salty-sweet, with a strong soy sauce taste, and proper yìnguā (on the right) has a light, delicate flavor and is distinctly sweet. This is due mainly to differences in the soy sauce used, so make sure you're using light soy sauce for jiàngguā, and white soy sauce for yìnguā. Unlike Japanese soy pickles, Taiwanese soy preserves don't use vinegar, so they will start to taste slightly sour only after a while due to fermentation and the interaction of the soy sauce and sugar.

蔭瓜 yìnguā | 蔭瓜仔 ìm-kue-á

Oriental Pickling Melons in White Soy Sauce

Crunchy-tender oriental pickling melons (opposite, right) are good to eat as is, like jiàngguā (Cucumbers in Sweet Soy Sauce, page 47), but are even better when used in cooking, such as for braising and in soups. They are packed with *kam-tinn* (甘甜) flavor.

Makes one 3-cup jar

4 lb (1,800g) oriental pickling melon 越瓜 or peeled ripe muskmelons 香瓜/美濃瓜

Salt

¾ cup white soy sauce, preferably Taiwanese black bean white soy sauce 黑豆白蔭油

¼ cup (50g) white rock sugar

½ cup Taiwanese rice cooking wine, preferably 19.5 percent ABV

2 pieces gan cao (dried licorice root) 甘草

1 Trim the ends of the melons and halve them lengthwise. With a spoon, scoop out and discard the pith and seeds. Weigh the melons and multiple that number by 2 percent—that is the weight of the salt you need. Place the melons in a large bowl, sprinkle with the salt, and massage it gently onto every surface.

2 Move the melons to a tofu cloth or cheesecloth and twist the cloth tightly to pack them together. Place the cloth into the large bowl and weigh it down with heavy weights (about 10 kg or 25 lb) for 1 day, until the melons easily bend into a U shape and reduce to about 600g in weight.

3 Take the melons out of the tofu cloth and dry their surfaces with a paper towel. Cut them into 2- to 2½-inch chunks. Lay them out in a single layer on a bamboo drying basket or steel tray and place them in the sun for 6 to 8 hours (or in a 150°F / 65°C oven for 1 to 2 hours), until they wrinkle and are a pale green color.

4 Add the melons, white soy sauce, rock sugar, rice cooking wine, and gan cao to a large pot. Bring to a gentle boil before covering, reducing the heat, and simmering for 1½ hours, until the melons are just tender but still have a slight bite.

5 Let the melons cool slightly, then pour everything into a lidded 4-cup glass container. Store in the refrigerator for at least 2 days before using. Store refrigerated for up to 2 months.

醬鳳梨 jiàngfènglí | 王梨醬 ông-lâi-tsiùnn

Pineapple in Soybean Sauce

My trip to the soybean artisans in the Daxi District in Taoyuan City inspired me to make these two jars. Ms. Huang, a fourth-generation bean-curd maker, uses all kinds of handmade soybean and soy sauce preserves to enrich her dishes. In her cupboard, she keeps a supercharged soy sauce made from blending fermented bean curd in soy sauce. When we were cooking together, she told me to flavor my braised tofu with it. "Squirt a little in, but don't add too much," she reminded me. "It's very rich!" I watched as she held a freshly picked bamboo shoot in her palm and shaved slices directly into water, then dropped in strips of yìnguā (Oriental Pickling Melons in White Soy Sauce, page 49). "These two ingredients are all you need," she said as she held up a spoonful for me to taste. "See, isn't it sweet and refreshing?" The key to good soup, I thought as the umami broth lingered on my tongue, lies in jiàngcài (preserved vegetables).

For this recipe, you'll want a pineapple that is ripe but not too ripe, marked mostly yellow on the skin with some traces of green. Too underripe and you won't get that intoxicating pineapple aroma unique to this preserve; too overripe, the pieces will become soft and mushy. This ferment is meant to bring a pleasing acidity to dishes, so look for pineapples that are slightly more tart than sweet. You can save the pineapple core to cook in broths; it adds a very nice floral sweetness!

Makes one 4-cup jar

1 peeled and cored pineapple (600g), cut into 1-inch chunks

Salt, preferably a coarse non-iodized pickling salt

¼ cup (50g) soybean koji 豆麴/豆粕

3 Tbsp Taiwanese rice cooking wine, or enough to cover, plus more for rinsing, preferably 19.5 percent ABV

½ cup (100g) golden granulated sugar

4 pieces gan cao (dried licorice root) 甘草

1 Weigh the pineapple chunks and multiply that number by 10 percent—that is the total weight of the salt you need. Place the pineapple chunks in a large bowl and toss them with half of the total salt. Let sit for 2 hours. You should see lots of liquid seep out.

2 Rinse the koji with about 2 Tbsp rice cooking wine for a few seconds to get rid of any dust or impurities. You don't want to rinse them too well, as you'll be washing away some of the koji spores as well. Pick out any discolored or damaged soybeans. Drain the soybean koji and add it to a medium mixing bowl. Stir in the sugar and the remaining salt.

3 Rinse a lidded 3-cup glass container with about 1 Tbsp rice cooking wine and pour it out. Pack a layer of the soybean mixture into the bottom of the container. Follow with a layer of pineapple chunks and repeat so you get alternating layers of each. Pack the chunks in a way that allows all sides of the pineapple to have contact with the soybeans. The top layer should be the soybean mixture. Rinse the gan cao gently with a little rice cooking wine and add those to the soybean layer. Top everything with the pineapple liquid and rice cooking wine. There should be enough liquid to cover everything.

4 Secure the lid and let ferment at room temperature out of direct sunlight for 3 months. Refrigerate after opening and store for up to 2 years.

甜酒豆腐乳 tiánjiǔ dòufǔrǔ | 豆乳 tāu-lú
Sweet Wine Fermented Bean Curd

A fermented bean curd laced with soybeans and sweet rice wine (see page 51 photograph, right) is typical in Taiwanese homes. It has the texture of cream cheese and a sweet, decadent savory flavor that makes a versatile condiment for stir-frying and dissolving in broths, like shàngtāng (Superior Stock, page 151). Besides nibbling on it with congee, many people love spreading it on toast and plain steamed buns. This is different from the "spicy fermented bean curd in sesame oil," which I sometimes call for, a nutty and funky version that you'll be able to find in most Asian grocery stores.

Note: Some specialty shops sell dried tofu cubes called dòufǔjiǎo (豆腐角), which are already salted and dried for making fermented bean curd. If you're lucky enough to find those, you can skip the dehydration steps below.

Makes one 3-cup jar

1 (400g) block medium-firm tofu 板豆腐

Salt

½ cup (100g) soybean koji 豆麴／豆粕

½ cup (120g) rice koji 米麴

¾ cup Taiwanese rice cooking wine, or enough to cover, plus about ½ cup more for rinsing, preferably 19.5 percent ABV

1 cup (200g) golden granulated sugar

1 Preheat the oven to 150°F (65°C). Line a baking tray with parchment paper.

2 Drain and pat dry the block of tofu before cutting it into nine 1¼- to 1½-inch cubes. Weigh the tofu and multiply that number by 15 percent—that is the weight of the salt you need. In a small dish, place the salt. Dip each side of every tofu cube in the salt, then place them one by one on the prepared baking tray. By the end, you should have used up all the salt.

3 Dehydrate the tofu cubes in the oven for 6 to 7 hours, flipping them halfway through, until the tofu is yellow in color and hardened significantly but with a slight spring. Remove them from the oven but leave the oven on.

4 Line a plate with a few paper towels. In a large pot, bring 5 cups water to a boil. Tap off any surface salt from the dried tofu cubes and slide them into the boiling water, blanching for 3 minutes to parcook the tofu and

rid it of excess salt. Using a spider strainer, remove the tofu and transfer them to the paper towel–lined plate to drain. Line the baking tray with a new piece of parchment paper and place the blanched tofu cubes on it. Place in the oven for 25 to 30 minutes more, until their surfaces are once again fully dry. Set aside to cool to room temperature.

5 Meanwhile, mix the soybean and rice koji in a bowl. Rinse with ¼ to ½ cup of rice cooking wine for a few seconds to get rid of any dust or impurities. You don't want them too clean as you'll be washing away some of the koji spores as well. Pick out any discolored or damaged koji. Drain the koji and add it to a medium bowl. Stir in the sugar and set aside.

6 Rinse a lidded 3-cup glass container with about 1 Tbsp rice cooking wine and pour it out. Pack a layer of the koji mixture into the bottom of the container. Follow with a layer of tofu and repeat so you get alternating layers of each. Pack the cubes in a way that allows all sides of the tofu cubes to have contact with the koji mixture. The top layer should be the koji mixture. Top with the rice cooking wine to just cover everything.

7 Secure the lid and let the mixture ferment at room temperature and out of direct sunlight for 3 months. The color will darken as it sits. Refrigerate after opening and store for up to 2 years.

Variation: Pineapple and Red Yeast Rice Flavor

Replace the soybean koji with more rice koji. In the koji-sugar mixture, reduce the sugar to ½ cup (100g), add 4 tsp (12g) red yeast rice, and add ¼ head peeled and cored pineapple (120g), cut into ½-inch-thick slices.

Vegetarian Meat

Liánhuāyàn (蓮花宴), named after the pink lotus that Dizang Buddha sits on, is the most elaborate of religious banquets at the monastery. That's when the nuns emptied their supply of mock meats for a flood of non-vegetarian, recently grieving visitors. I went with my parents one month after A-Gong passed. Every dish there was plated based on the different parts and stages of a blossom. You saw a platter of lion's head meatballs in concentric arrangements of bok choy; thin sheets of matsutake mushroom layered over braised vegetables like a not yet bloomed bud, awaiting maturity; and a mock shark fin casserole with bell peppers in as many colors as the flowers on A-Má's gaudy dress.

When I began writing this book, I looked back at the pictures I took from that banquet. I didn't remember how the dishes tasted. My interest in vegetarian cooking took root after I left Taiwan. The dishes I tasted before, in the funeral processions that I tried to forget about, were inevitably shy of wholeness when I attempted to exhume their memory.

I thought a lot about a particular fried vegetarian fish that the nuns made. They wrapped slivers of tofu skin in nori sheets, deep-fried the whole thing, and smothered it with a smooth, glossy reddish-orange sweet-and-sour sauce. The nori pressed against the tofu skin casing looked rugged, like fish scales. I thought it was an aesthetically perfect dish. It just needed to taste more like fish. I blended kombu and wakame seaweed into small flecks and mixed them into the tofu skin with heaps of grated ginger, in hopes of drowning out the soy flavors. It worked as it should and tasted great, but I still felt vaguely unsatisfied. The fish never got "fishy" enough. Once, I had a chance to consult the auntie at the tofu vendor in the morning market. I recited to her my exact process and intentions. She almost immediately frowned, and told me that the vegetarian fish was never supposed to taste like fish. The dish harkened to sānshēng (三牲), the three traditional animal sacrifices for venerating the dead: pig, chicken, and fish. In a Buddhist vegetarian household, offering something shaped like a fish as validation for piety was the extent to which it needed to pretend to be what it's not.

麥面筋 miànjīn | 麥面麥齊 mī-thi

Wheat Gluten

Wheat gluten is essentially texture, a chewy blank canvas. Like tofu, it can take on many forms through different shaping and cooking techniques. It is less absorbent than tofu but will still take in any flavors you put it with—given enough time. Feel free to take your gluten beyond the scope of this book. I like making the dough by hand and letting my senses guide me. I realize that, depending on the strength of your arms, kneading 4 pounds of dough may take considerable energy, so know that you can also do everything in a stand mixer.

Note: Don't forget the salt! Salt not only seasons but strengthens the gluten so you can stretch it significantly without it snapping in half.

1 In a very large mixing bowl, combine the flour and salt. Add the water and stir with chopsticks until you get something shaggy and light that resembles snowflakes. Set the chopsticks aside and start mixing the dough with your hands. The dough may feel too dry at first, but that's only because it takes time for this amount of flour to hydrate. If the dough refuses to come together, you can add a little bit more water. Continue to mix and knead for 2 to 3 minutes, until the dough is soft and slightly sticky. Cover the bowl with a damp cloth and let it rest for about 20 minutes to begin gluten development.

2 Move the dough to a lightly floured work surface. Knead for 8 to 10 minutes, until smooth, soft, and elastic. Think about building the gluten in one direction—use your body weight to roll the dough, then fold it, and repeat. Knead until you get sufficient gluten development. To test this, tear off a small piece of dough and stretch it. You should be able to stretch the piece to a paper-thin, three-finger-wide film that light can pass through. Place the dough back into the bowl and re-cover the bowl with a damp cloth. Let it rest for 30 minutes.

Makes 600g to 640g (21 to 22½ oz)

10 cups (1,200g) all-purpose flour, preferably with 11.5 percent-plus protein, plus more for dusting

1 tsp (6g) salt

3 cups (720g) water

3 Fit a large sieve in the bowl and place the dough into the sieve (see opposite). Move the bowl to the sink and begin washing out the wheat starch under running water. Knead the dough to facilitate the washing. Keep kneading and swirling the dough under the running water. The dough will gradually shrink and feel springier. Some pieces may separate from the main dough but should quickly reassemble when you gather them back together.

4 Stop kneading once the water runs mostly clear and the dough weighs roughly a third of its original weight (about 1,925g) and takes on a rugged, bouncy texture and off-white color, which should take 5 to 7 minutes.

5 Place the wheat gluten in a medium bowl and cover it with water. Cover and refrigerate for at least 2 hours and preferably overnight or up to 2 days, until smooth and much more elastic. Pour out and discard the water in the bowl and proceed to make Gluten Intestine (page 58), Gluten Threads (page 59), and/or Gluten Puffs (page 60).

Variation: Vital Wheat Gluten Version

In a large bowl, combine 2 cups (240g) vital wheat gluten, ¼ cup (60g) all-purpose flour, and 1 tsp salt. In a separate bowl, mix 1½ cups (360g) water with 2 tsp rice vinegar or distilled vinegar, and pour this into the dry ingredients. Knead for 5 to 7 minutes. Place the kneaded vital wheat gluten into a bowl with enough water to cover and soak overnight before using.

麵腸 miàncháng | 麵炙 mī-tsià
Gluten Intestine

Without being shaped, wheat gluten doesn't have a pleasing texture. Stretching and wrapping the gluten creates layers, just as with any laminated dough. These boiled gluten rolls get their name from their intestine-like appearance and chewy, tender texture. Chop, dice, or tear the gluten intestine apart with your hands and use it as a pork substitute. Frying it briefly in some hot oil gives the illusion of a fatty cut of meat, and it's a technique I use a lot in this book. If you don't wish to use any oil to cook it, you can also cut it on a diagonal bias and serve it with Garlic Soy Paste (page 101) or your desired sauce for a simple source of protein.

Makes 6
(about 100g each)

21 oz (600g) Wheat Gluten
(page 56)

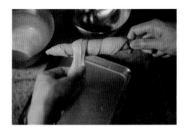

1 Place the wheat gluten on a wet cutting board. Stretch the wheat gluten into a 6-inch-long rectangle, and cut it into six 1-inch-wide batons. If the pieces lose their stretch after cutting them, set them aside for 10 minutes.

2 Leaving a small gap at the tip of a pair of chopsticks, wrap the short side of the gluten around the chopsticks in a spiral motion toward the other end. When you've used up about two-thirds of the gluten's length, wrap it in a reverse spiral back up toward the middle of the roll. Press the wheat gluten tightly to adhere the loose end. Carefully push and slide the completed gluten intestine off the pair of chopsticks. Set the rolled-up gluten aside on a plate or tray; repeat with the remaining pieces.

3 Bring a pot of water to a gentle boil over medium-high heat. Add the gluten intestines and boil for 10 to 12 minutes, until they float. Drain and let cool completely.

4 If you're not using these the same day, pack them into resealable bags and freeze for up to 3 months. Thaw completely before using.

皮絲 písī

Gluten Threads

Dehydrating gluten in hot oil makes it stiff and chewy like lean meat, so this is sometimes called vegetarian duck (sùyāròu 素鴨肉). Soak the gluten threads in hot water for 30 to 40 minutes before use, until it becomes soft and pliable. You can chop the gluten threads to make something like a textured vegetable protein mince or keep it whole like slabs of meat and cook it in more heavily flavored broths.

Note: If you're lucky enough to be in Taiwan, you can find gluten threads sold at most vegetarian vendors. They are fried until very dry to make them shelf-stable, so you'll need to soak them overnight before use.

1 Dig your thumb into the top-center of the gluten intestine and pry it open to reveal its layers. Work downward until you have a whole, flat sheet of gluten with lots of exposed nooks and crannies. Tear each piece in half crosswise and set aside.

2 In a wok over medium heat, warm the neutral oil to 248°F (120°C). Add the gluten and fry steadily for 30 to 40 minutes, until just golden with no more off-white-colored spots. Using a spider strainer or slotted spoon, move the gluten threads onto a paper towel–lined plate and set them aside to drain.

3 Bring the oil up to 300°F (150°C). Fry the gluten threads for 8 to 10 minutes more, until fully dehydrated and a dark golden brown. Remove the gluten threads and drain them on the paper towel–lined plate. Store in the refrigerator for up to 3 months.

Makes 6
(about 25g each)

3 Gluten Intestines
(page 58; 300g total)

About 2 cups neutral oil,
for frying

麵筋泡 miànjīnpào

Gluten Puffs

Shaping and frying the wheat gluten into little balls creates hollow puffs (see photograph on page 55). Their texture is like fried tofu skin, except they retain their chew even after cooking for a while. Before using them, submerge the gluten puffs in hot water; they should instantly deflate and be ready for cooking. They're great braised in soy sauce, like in the breakfast classic tǔdòu miànjīn (Braised Gluten with Peanuts, page 68), and added to stir-fries for their chewy, fried egg–like texture.

Makes 30
(about 200g total)

10½ oz (300g) Wheat Gluten (page 56)

2 cups neutral oil, for frying

1 Fill a baking tray with a shallow layer of water. Roll and stretch the wheat gluten into a roughly 30-inch-length log, then divide it with a knife or scissors into 30 equal thumb-size pieces, about 10g each. If you have a digital scale, use it! It's crucial that all the pieces are similar in size so they fry evenly. Roll each piece into a smooth ball and place them into the water-filled baking tray.

2 In a wok over medium heat, warm the neutral oil to 250°F (120°C). Add 8 to 10 gluten balls (do not overcrowd the wok) and immediately move the gluten balls around to minimize sticking. Adjust the heat to medium-high and use tongs or a pair of chopsticks to gently but swiftly turn the balls over and over. As they start to float, push them back down into the oil with a spider strainer. Even heating is key here—you want them to puff up as much as possible before the outer layer is set. Continue to fry for 5 to 8 minutes, until the oil temperature reaches 320°F (160°C), then lower the heat to medium or medium-low to keep the oil at this temperature. Fry for a few more minutes until golden and completely set. To check the progress, lift the gluten balls up from the oil with a slotted spoon or spider strainer. If they collapse immediately (or within 30 seconds), the center is not adequately dehydrated yet.

3 Once the center is set, using a slotted spoon or spider strainer, transfer the gluten puffs onto a wire rack to cool. Repeat with the remaining dough. Store the fried puffs in the refrigerator for up to 2 months.

 **dòujī**

Soy Chicken

When wrapped tight and steamed, fresh tofu skin coalesces to make this imitation chicken product. Slice it up to get something nice and succulent like dòugān (豆乾, bean curd). Tear the soy chicken with your hands for more textured chunks, similar to chicken thighs.

Makes 2
(about 200g each)

14 oz (400g) fresh tofu skin rolls 豆包

2 (10 by 10-inch) sheets dried tofu skin 千張/腐皮

1 Slice the fresh tofu skin rolls along the grain into 4 by ¼-inch strands. Squeeze out any excess water and pat them dry.

2 Place half of the tofu skin strands onto one sheet of the dried tofu skin. Pack the strands tightly and form a 5-inch column at the bottom third of the dried tofu skin, leaving an equal spacing on each side (left and right) and about 1½ inches at the bottom. Lift the bottom end of the dried tofu skin up and over the column, just as you would wrap a burrito. Fold in the side flaps and roll it tightly to seal. Move the roll seam-side down to the bottom center of a roughly 12 by 12-inch piece of glass paper or parchment paper. Roll in a similar fashion—fold up the bottom and the sides and roll it tightly. Wrap the roll again in a linen or tofu cloth and roll tightly once more.

3 Take a 5-foot-long kitchen twine and bite one end of the twine to give the twine some tension. Wrap the twine twice around the center of the roll. You want the twine to be wrapped very tightly—do this with as much force as possible. Veer the twine 1½ inches to the right and wrap it two or three times. Veer the twine to the left, 1½ inches from the center, and wrap it two or three times. Veer the twine back toward the middle and tie it in a knot with the starting end of the twine. Repeat with the remaining half of the fresh tofu skins and the remaining sheet of dried tofu skin.

4 Place the roll in a bamboo steamer (or a steel steamer or metal steaming stand). Set the steamer over a large pot of boiling water and steam on high for 30 minutes. Remove the wrapping and let the soy chicken cool completely. If you're not using it the same day, pack into resealable bags and freeze for up to 3 months. Thaw completely before using.

猴頭菇 hóutóugū | kâu-thâu-koo

Lion's Mane Mushrooms

Dried lion's mane mushrooms are meatier in texture than fresh ones but need a source of protein to make their fibers less stale and woody. Taiwanese tradition calls for soaking the mushrooms in beaten eggs or powdered egg whites. Below is a method that the Buddhist nuns use to keep them eggless—soy protein powder and a brief fry—and the result is even more fragrant, and "Q" (springy). Use whenever you need a chicken or beef substitute in stir-fries, braises, or soups.

Makes about 2 lb (900g)

10½ oz (300g) dried lion's mane mushrooms

6 Tbsp (30g) soy protein isolate

2 tsp Mushroom Powder 香菇粉 (page 15) or store-bought

3½ cups water

4 cups neutral oil, for frying

1 Place the dried lion's mane mushrooms in a large bowl and cover with room-temperature water. Place a plate and a weight over the bowl to keep the mushrooms submerged. Let them soak and rehydrate for 1 hour, or until fully soft and easily torn by hand.

2 Inspect the mushrooms for any black or discolored spots, using scissors to remove them. Trim off and discard the thicker, harder stems. Cut the mushrooms into 1-inch chunks that resemble broccoli florets. In the same large bowl, soak the mushrooms in new water for 1 more hour, squeezing the water from the mushrooms and changing the water every 15 minutes. The water will get clearer as you soak and change the waters. This is a sign that the bitter, unpleasant flavors are leaving.

3 Bring a large pot of water to a rolling boil over high heat. Add the hydrated mushrooms and boil for 3 to 5 minutes, until no longer bitter (taste a small piece to check). If there is still a bitter aftertaste, drain the mushrooms, bring a new pot of water to a boil, and repeat the blanching process.

4 Drain and rinse the mushrooms under running water until cool to the touch. Take your time with this; mushrooms are great at retaining heat, and you don't want to scald yourself when squeezing out the water! Squeeze the mushrooms to remove as much liquid as possible.

5 On a cutting board and with a heavy rolling pin or the flat side of a
   cleaver, lightly smack the mushrooms one by one to release the fibers
   and tenderize them until they are ¼ to ½ inch thick.

6 In a large mixing bowl, whisk together the soy protein isolate,
   mushroom powder, and the water. Whisk until no lumps remain and
   then transfer all the smacked mushrooms to this bowl. Let soak in the
   refrigerator for at least 12 hours and up to 24 hours.

7 Spread the mushrooms out in a parchment-lined, 9-inch bamboo steamer
   or a steamer of choice. Set the steamer over a large pot of boiling water
   and steam on high for 40 minutes. Remove the mushrooms and let them
   cool completely before squeezing out any excess water.

8 Line a large plate with paper towels. In a wok over medium-high heat,
   warm the neutral oil until the temperature reaches about 250°F (120°C).
   Add the lion's mane mushrooms and fry for 3 to 5 minutes, until the
   hairs of the mushrooms are golden brown. Using a spider strainer or
   slotted spoon, transfer the mushrooms to the paper towel–lined plate to
   drain. Cool completely. If not using them the same day, pack the fried
   mushrooms into separate resealable bags for ease of access and freeze for
   up to 6 months.

Breakfast

I owe my yearning for traditional flavors to A-Gong, who saw food as more than just sustenance. He was moved by the way food derives meaning from people and their lives. The dishes he considered to be *kóo-tsá bī* (古早味)—old-time flavors—in particular held a special place in his heart, because he'd witnessed them float and sink under the confluence of cultures and people on this island.

A-Gong had a distinctly Taiwanese palate; it's almost as if traditional food was all he could

apple-crisp cucumbers pickled in sweet soy, and a tiny yet pungent cube of fermented bean curd.

His partiality stems from childhood memory. When he was a little kid, Japanese colonists ruled over Taiwan. Airstrike alarms and hissing bombs were an everyday experience; they shrieked and split the clouds like thunder, he said, and he and his siblings would duck and dash toward the shelters whenever they heard the sounds. Because the Japanese military requisitioned grains from the people, rice shortages occurred everywhere. Mornings were filled with the smells not of freshly cooked rice, but of sweet potatoes, whose abundance in a time of poverty and famine maligned it with such. Like many families, his mother stewed the tubers with the dwindling amount of rice they had. Some days, with his fingers alone he could count the number of grains floating in the soup.

I remember his memory puzzled me at first—the mere sight of congee and sweet potatoes, I thought, should've been a horrible reminder of the pain he and his family had endured. Some of his peers trembled at the sight because of the trauma of that past. He told me otherwise: he ate it because it made him feel like he was sitting at his mom's table again. When the world seemed to be collapsing around him, the steam from the hot congee reassured him that he would not be alone even if it did. It was those tender feelings of nourishment that prevailed, not the limitation, hardship, or suffering.

For the seventeen years that I had known A-Gong, he never went a day without his breakfast congee. Even on vacation, he carried a diànguō (rice cooker) with him to make his congee in the hotel. I suppose we can all find a little meaning and comfort in our morning routines, lest we get lost in them.

stomach. He was quite particular about everything. His breakfast sweet potato congee was one of those things. The rice had to be cooked soft but not split, the ám (泔, the starchy rice liquid that gathers on top) thick and shimmering, and the sweet potato chunks—half a fist-size each—had to have the perfect bite, tender and gently sweet. The bowl had to be surrounded by a spread of jiàngcài (Preserved Vegetables, page 30) sides—incomplete without a heaped dish of salty minced preserved radishes,

番薯糜 han-tsî-bê

Sweet Potato Congee

Distinct, intact rice grains, A-Gong would say, is where the Minnan *bê* (糜) separates from Cantonese *zhōu* (粥), where the grains melt into one another. The body of the congee won't taste like sweet potatoes, and I quite like the heterogeneity; you can shave or cut one of the sweet potatoes into strips if you'd like it to impart a stronger flavor. Some sweet potato varieties take longer to cook than others, so experiment. In Taiwan, with the golden "No. 57" sweet potatoes, I add the rice five minutes before adding the sweet potatoes. In California, I generally have to add the sweet potatoes ten minutes before adding the rice.

Serves 6

1 cup (240g) short-grain white rice

6 small yellow-fleshed sweet potatoes (600g total weight)

12½ cups water

1   In a medium bowl, rinse the white rice three to five times, until the water runs mostly clear. Drain and set the rice aside.

2   Peel the sweet potatoes by first removing the outer skin, then the white layer underneath the skin. Don't skimp here. The white layer can turn gray as the sweet potato cooks, which will give it an unappetizing look. Slice them crosswise in half on a bias or cut them into chunks 2 to 3 inches in length.

3   Bring the water to a rolling boil over high heat in a tall pot. Add the white rice and sweet potatoes. Lower the heat to medium or medium-low so the water is bubbling gently. Cover partially and cook for about 30 minutes, stirring occasionally to make sure nothing is stuck to the sides or bottom of the pot, until all the grains are soft, the liquid is a thickened pearlescent white, and a paring knife pierces the potatoes without resistance. The congee may appear too thin at this point, but it will thicken a lot as it rests. Cover the pot with a lid. Turn off the heat and let the congee stand to allow the rice and *ám* (the starchy soup) to meld together for 15 to 30 minutes and no more than 1 hour before serving. Serve with a spread of your choice of sides.

土豆麵筋 tǔdòu miànjīn | 土豆麥面麥离 thôo-tāu-mī-thi

Braised Gluten with Peanuts

The canned food aisle in Taiwanese supermarkets always fascinated me as a kid. I could spend hours inspecting the colorful jars, judging each one as if it was in a beauty pageant. This dish is inspired by one of those jars always enshrined on the supermarket shelves, a certified congee killer and all-star side dish: chewy tender gluten puffs braised in sweet soy sauce, bursting with juices and an intoxicating peanut aroma. See the photograph on page 66.

Makes one 3-cup jar

½ cup (100g) shelled whole raw peanuts

½ cup (15g) mini dried shiitake mushrooms

4 (1½-inch) pieces kombu (5g)

4½ oz (125g) Gluten Puffs 麵筋泡 (page 60) or use store-bought

Neutral oil for frying

3 Tbsp (38g) yellow rock sugar

1 Tbsp Taiwanese rice cooking wine

¼ cup light soy sauce

¼ tsp salt

1 In a small bowl, soak the peanuts in water to cover for 1 hour. Drain the peanuts. In a small pot, bring 2 to 3 cups water to a gentle boil. Add the peanuts and cook for 30 to 45 minutes, until the peanuts are soft and starchy on the inside but still have a bite. Drain and set aside.

2 Bring a medium pot with 2 cups water to a boil, then remove it from the heat. Add the mushrooms and kombu, cover to keep warm, and soak for at least 1 hour. Using a slotted spoon or spider strainer, remove the mushrooms when they're needed and the kombu when the broth is needed.

3 Bring a separate medium pot with 6 cups water to a rolling boil. Add the gluten puffs and blanch for about 1 minute, until they have all shrunk and collapsed. Set the gluten puffs aside.

4 In a medium pot over medium heat, warm 1 tsp of neutral oil. Add the shiitake mushrooms and fry to release their fragrance, 1 to 2 minutes. Stir in the gluten puffs and peanuts. Add the rock sugar, rice cooking wine, and soy sauce and cook for about 1 minute, stirring the ingredients together, until very fragrant. Add the broth (without the kombu) and season with the salt. Bring to a gentle boil, cover partially, and braise for 1 hour. At the end, taste and adjust the seasonings as needed. Remove the pot from the heat and let cool completely.

5 Ladle everything into a lidded 3-cup glass container. Secure the lid and store in the refrigerator for at least 1 day before enjoying. Store in the refrigerator for up to 2 months.

On today's Taipei streets, you won't walk long before coming across a zǎocāndiàn (breakfast stall). Every neighborhood has their own, a hub for soy milk and hearty, wheat flour–heavy pastries. It's the epicenter of the neighborhood's ecosystem, a place where people start—and sometimes end—their days. You sit at the stall in the morning sky's dim ambiance, take a sip of something warm, watch the clouds part, and the world become beautiful.

Even though many of today's iconic Taiwanese breakfast items contain wheat, their popularity is a more recent development. Traditionally, breakfast consisted of mostly rice and rice-based dishes. When the democratic Republic of China (ROC) government fell to the communists in 1949, the ROC government leaders and 1.2 million mainland Chinese (mostly northerners) fled to Taiwan and brought their appetite for wheat flour–based dishes with them.

A few years later, In 1954, US president Dwight Eisenhower signed Public Law 480, which allowed Taiwan to purchase flour cheaply from the United States. The new ROC government was also incentivized to push the new grains on the Taiwanese to remind them of pre-communist China's glory. There was suddenly both a demand and supply for it, and mainlander cooks started crafting and selling the wheat flour–based foods they knew from home. Chinese technique cross-pollinated with local produce, and a new genre of Taiwanese-style wheat flour–based foods was created. Due to industrialization, fewer people were cooking and eating at home in the morning, and these wheat-based foods were cheap, filling, and convenient. They soon prevailed as the breakfast items of choice. Breakfast stalls began to pop up all over the island, serving the traditional breakfast we see there today.

車窗擊破牀

Window Breaker In Case of Em

豆漿 dòujiāng | 豆奶 tāu-ni
Soy Milk

Fresh, hot bowls of dòujiāng (soy milk) are the hallmarks of a Taiwanese breakfast stall, but the best soy milk I've ever had is from the Buddhist monastery. Every time I volunteered there, the nuns would pour me a hot cup, and I'd sip and savor it before we started cooking.

Watching the nuns make soy milk is a quick way to understand what Buddhists mean when they say cooking is ascetic training. Great dòujiāng is velvety smooth, nutty, and naturally sweet—a transcending experience. Their handmade process requires a trained eye and is both precise and fluid. "It's all about experience," says Huìqiáo Shifu, the nun in charge of operations. After a decade of tofu making, she still logs the results and parameters of each take. She dips her pinkie into the dòujiāng, gets a quick taste, and knows what proportions and temperatures she needs to adjust for the day's batch. She then goes on to turn the elixir into perfect squares of dòubāo (tofu skin), dòufǔ (tofu), and dòugān (bean curd).

Freshly made dòujiāng, unlike most cartons of American soy milk, is not meant to be a dairy substitute. It tastes distinctly beany and *will* curdle hot coffee. If you hope to incorporate drinking soy milk into your daily routine, I recommend investing in an automatic soy milk maker, which is designed to grind and cook the beans into silky-smooth soy milk.

Note: Try to use soft water or distilled water instead of hard water, which has a higher mineral content (specifically of calcium and magnesium) that, in significant amounts, can affect taste and coagulation. "The good taste of our tofu owes a large part to the purity of our water," say the nuns. "The water is filtered four or five times before we use it for our soy milk." The quality of your soybeans will also impact the taste and texture of your

Makes about 4 cups

1½ cups (300g) dried soybeans, about 680g after soaking

6¼ cups water, preferably soft water (see Note)

soy milk. Source the highest quality, organic, and non-GMO soybeans you can find. It's a two-ingredient recipe, after all.

1 Add the soybeans to a medium bowl. Gently rinse and pick out any bad or discolored ones and then fill the bowl with enough water to cover them by 2 inches. Soak for 5 to 7 hours in the summer and 10 to 12 hours in the winter, until they are twice their original size. To check the soaking progress, pick a soybean up and pinch it with your nails. When ready, it should easily split in half, revealing a full, not concave, even light-yellow interior.

2 Drain the soybeans. In a high-speed blender, blend the soybeans and 4 cups of the water on high until very, very fine, 6 to 10 minutes, depending on the power of your blender.

3 In a tall pot, bring the remaining 2¼ cups water to a boil over medium-high heat. The pot should be tall enough so that the soy milk reaches only halfway up the pot. Transfer the blended soybean mixture to the pot. Ladle some liquid from the pot back into the blender, pulse it a few times to rinse, and add that back into the pot. Stir the soy milk to thoroughly mix it and continue to stir until the whole pot comes to a boil again. About 1 minute into the boil, you will feel that a layer has stuck to the bottom. This is very normal when you heat raw soy milk for the first time—no matter how vigorously you stir, a layer of solids will still precipitate out and begin to caramelize. The layer is nearly impossible to scrape up, will very quickly burn, and can give the whole pot a burnt taste. Pour all the soy milk into another large, tall pot, leaving behind the layer on the bottom, and cook over medium-high heat, stirring continuously. Another layer, albeit thinner, may gather on the bottom. This is fine. Leave the layer alone, lower the heat slightly, continue to cook, and stir the soy milk slightly above that layer. If you have another tall pot or can have someone scrub the original pot, you can transfer the soy milk once more to be extra safe.

(continued)

4 Continue to heat the soy milk so that it comes to a rolling boil. With the thick and heavy foam on top, it will be difficult to tell by visual cues whether the soy milk has truly boiled or not. Use a thermometer to check—the temperature should register 207°F (97°C). Lower the heat to low and continue to cook, stirring, for 10 minutes more. Taste the soy milk—if it is grassy at all, cook for about another 5 minutes.

5 Line another large pot with a tofu cloth or cheesecloth. Pour the cooked soy milk through the cloth, pull up all four corners, and twist it to form a bag. Strain the soy milk by slinging the heavy pulp around the pot and pressing it against the sides of the pot (be careful, it'll be very hot!) until little to no liquid comes out. If your cloth is fine enough, the soy milk should be very smooth without perceivable mealy bits on your tongue (or very few).

6 Pour the strained soy milk into a lidded jug and store it in the refrigerator for up to 2 days. To serve, sweeten the soy milk to taste. Or, keep it unsweetened like I do.

Variation: Black Soybean Milk (hēidòujiāng 黑豆漿)

Use 1¼ cups (250 g) dried black soybeans (preferably with a green kernel, 青仁黑豆) and ¼ cup (50 g) regular dried soybeans. Swapping some of the yellow soybeans for black soybeans promotes an earthier, nuttier taste, and as the nuns would say, aids to improve circulation. Follow the instructions for blending and cooking in the preceding recipe. You can play with the proportions and yield different tastes.

鹹豆漿 xiándòujiāng | 鹹豆奶 kiâm-tāu-ni

Savory Soy Milk

When seasoned with savory ingredients and curdled with rice vinegar, soy milk can almost mimic silky steamed eggs. The key here is balance. Use just enough rice vinegar to coagulate the soy milk and keep a hint of its fragrance, but not enough to sour it. Season with just enough salt, soy sauce, and preserved mustard to bring out the natural flavors of the soy milk, but not enough to overpower it. The texture you get depends on your soy milk: the finer and more concentrated it is, the more custard-like it becomes. Top with vegetarian meat floss for a nice extra touch. See the photograph on page 64.

1 In a small bowl, add the ingredients one by one in this order: preserved mustard, scallion, sugar, salt, light soy sauce, rice vinegar, sesame oil, and chili oil (if using).

2 In a small saucepan over medium-high heat, warm the soy milk, constantly swirling or stirring it to prevent the bottom from burning. Once the soy milk boils, pour it quickly and all at once (or from a relatively high point) into the serving bowl to make sure the vinegar and seasonings distribute throughout. The soy milk should set, almost instantly, into a soft custard.

3 Place the fried crullers on top. Serve immediately.

Serves 1

1 tsp minced preserved mustard 榨菜

1 small scallion, finely chopped

½ tsp golden granulated sugar

¼ tsp salt

1 tsp light soy sauce

¾ tsp rice vinegar

¼ tsp sesame oil 香油

¼ tsp Chili Oil (page 95; optional)

1¼ cups unsweetened soy milk 豆漿 (page 74)

1 (3-inch) piece Fried Crullers 油條 (page 85) or use store-bought, cut into 4 pieces

米漿 mǐjiāng | bí-tsiunn

Peanut Rice Milk

This thick and sweet rice milk is something in between a drink and a soup, like a peanut and rice congee blitzed into glossy smooth oblivion. The color of roasted peanuts is, as with roasted coffee beans, an indication of flavor and aroma. A light roast is golden, nutty, and perfect for something you'd snack on, but you'll want a dark roast for mǐjiāng. Prominent, glistening brown, and slightly burnt, a dark roast carries a fragrance and taste that can withstand dilution. I like mixing a few spoons into my soy milk as a peanut-flavored sweetener. See the photograph on page 64.

Serves 6

¼ cup (50g) brown rice or white rice

⅓ cup (80g) unsalted raw, shelled peanuts

4 cups water

⅓ cup (70g) golden granulated sugar, plus more as needed

Fried Crullers (page 85), for serving

1 In a medium bowl, rinse and drain the rice a few times. Cover the rice with water by about 1 inch. Soak at room temperature for at least 4 hours and up to overnight.

2 Preheat the oven to 355°F (180°C). Spread the peanuts in a single layer on a baking tray. Roast for 30 to 35 minutes, occasionally stirring, until the peanuts are dark brown, like a medium-roast coffee. Set aside.

3 Drain the rice. In a blender, combine the rice, roasted peanuts, and 2 cups of the water on high for 3 to 5 minutes, until completely smooth and no grainy bits remain.

4 Bring the remaining 2 cups water to a boil in a medium pot over medium-high heat. Set a fine-mesh sieve over the pot and pour the contents of the blender through it. Use a spoon to stir and lightly press on the mixture in the sieve, extracting as much liquid as possible. Discard the mealy pulp in the sieve. Bring the rice milk to a boil, stirring constantly. About a minute in, you will feel that a layer has stuck to the bottom. The layer is nearly impossible to scrape up and will very quickly burn. Pour all the rice milk into another large pot, leaving behind the layer on the bottom. Stir the sugar into the peanut milk, lower the heat to medium or medium-low, and simmer for 10 minutes. Taste and adjust the sweetness as desired. Serve as is or with fried crullers on the side for dipping. Store any leftovers in an airtight jar in the refrigerator for up to 5 days.

杏仁茶 xìngrénchá | hīng-lîn tê

Almond Tea

Before the dawn of soy milk, a hot velvety bowl of almond tea was the breakfast staple. This isn't almond milk; the "almond" in the name refers to the flat, pale kernels found in apricot pits. There are two kinds of apricot kernels: southern ("sweet") and northern ("bitter"). Cantonese people often mix both in their almond tea, but Taiwanese people prefer using only southern apricot kernels as they have a milder taste. In this recipe, unroasted peanuts supplant northern apricots with a background fragrance and richness that make this feel uniquely Taiwanese. See the photograph on page 64.

1 In a medium bowl, rinse and drain the apricot kernels and peanuts. Add just enough water to cover and soak at room temperature for at least 6 hours or up to overnight.

2 Drain the apricot kernels and peanuts. In a blender, blend the apricots, peanuts, and water on high until completely smooth and no grainy bits remain, 3 to 5 minutes.

3 Line a medium pot with a tofu cloth. Pour the apricot-peanut mixture through the cloth, pull up all four corners, and twist and squeeze the cloth as if wringing a towel, straining the liquid into the pot. Set the pot on the stove over medium-high heat. Bring the almond tea to a boil, constantly stirring, 3 to 5 minutes. Keep a close eye on this—bubbles will begin to form on the surface as it comes to a boil, and it can easily boil over. Add the sugar, stirring to dissolve. Lower the heat to a simmer and cook for an additional 10 minutes. The thick layer of foam on top should disappear as it boils. Taste and adjust the sweetness as desired.

4 Serve hot as is or with fried crullers on the side for dipping. Cool any leftovers and store in the refrigerator for up to 3 days.

Serves 6

1 cup (120g) southern apricot kernels 南杏

⅔ cup (120g) unsalted raw, shelled peanuts

4 cups water

¼ cup (50g) white rock sugar

Fried Crullers (page 85; optional), for serving

蛋餅 dànbǐng | 卵餅 nñg-piánn
Egg Crepes

This dànbǐng uses an old-school technique and is proof that, in the early 1950s, Taiwanese people suddenly had access to piles of flour but no idea how to use it. The chewy skin is based on a flour slurry—flour, sweet potato starch, and water stirred together—since they hadn't figured out how to knead dough yet. Eggless dànbǐng is virtually nonexistent on Taiwanese streets since many vegetarians here eat eggs. To make an eggless version, I typically use tofu skin, though I sometimes also use a liquid plant-based scramble. You don't have to keep it plain as I have here. Use the dànbǐng skin to wrap your favorite toppings—fried hash browns, sweet corn, cheese (or the plant-based equivalent), and vegetarian ham are mine.

Serves 1

Batter

¼ cup (30g) all-purpose flour

2 tsp (5g) fine sweet potato starch

⅛ tsp salt

⅓ cup water

1 small scallion, or 1 handful Taiwanese or Thai basil leaves 九層塔, finely chopped

Neutral oil for frying

Filling

2 oz (60g) fresh tofu skin rolls 豆包, roughly torn

Pinch of salt

-

Soy sauce paste or dòubànjiàng (chili bean paste) or chili sauce of choice for serving

1 To make the batter: In a medium bowl, combine the flour, sweet potato starch, and salt. Add the water and chopped scallions and combine, stirring with chopsticks until no clumps remain and a thin batter forms.

2 In a round nonstick pan (ideally about 10 inches in diameter) set over medium to medium-high heat, warm 1 tsp neutral oil. Add the batter and swiftly swirl the pan around to distribute the batter evenly. Don't worry about making a perfect circle; you'll be rolling it up anyway. The batter should quickly set and go from white to translucent, about 2 minutes. Flip to cook the other side until both sides have brown bubbly spots, 4 to 6 minutes total. Transfer to a large plate or cutting board.

3 To make the filling: While the dànbǐng is still hot, spread the tofu skin all over it. The residual heat of the dànbǐng should allow the tofu skin to adhere nicely. Sprinkle a pinch of salt on top to season the interior.

4 Roll the dànbǐng up tightly without pulling it too much to prevent tearing. Use a lightly oiled knife to cut the dànbǐng crosswise into six pieces. Serve immediately, with your sauces of choice on the side for dipping.

火燒食并 shāobǐng | sio-piánn

Sesame Flatbread

My dad is a huge fan of traditional breakfast, so when I was little, he went out early every Sunday to bring back shāobǐng stuffed with yóutiáo (Fried Crullers, page 85) for us. We ate in the comfort of our home and added our own fixings. I kept mine mostly plain, maybe with an extra fried egg and some meat floss. Dad liked his loaded like a sandwich, with heaps of lettuce, sliced tomatoes, avocados, sweet corn, and bacon. The shāobǐng from our favorite stalls had a contrast of textures: a mix of crunch and bend, rather than just flaky and brittle throughout. This recipe honors that experience. "Solid," as my dad would say, with crumbs stuck on his lips.

Note: Like pizza, shāobǐng gets its distinctive texture from a quick, hot bake. Traditionally, it's baked in a clay urn. If your oven doesn't go to 500°F (260°C), crank it to the highest heat possible. I recommend using a preheated pizza stone, as it mimics the instant lift you get from a traditional clay urn.

1 Place a pizza stone in the center of the oven and preheat to 500°F (260°C), or as high as you can, with convection if available.

2 To make the dough: In a large bowl, combine the flour and salt. Stream in the boiling water, stirring constantly and vigorously with chopsticks, until all of the water is added and the mixture is shaggy and light, resembling snowflakes. Let the mixture sit for 1 minute, then stir in the cold water, mixing until all of it is absorbed. Add the neutral oil and knead by hand to incorporate the ingredients until a dough just comes together, 2 to 3 minutes. The dough at this stage should be soft, sticky, and patchy. Cover with a damp towel and rest for 20 to 30 minutes to begin gluten development. Knead the dough in the bowl until smooth, 4 to 5 minutes. Cover and rest for another 30 minutes.

Makes 4 flatbreads

Dough

2¼ cups (270g) all-purpose flour

½ tsp salt

½ cup plus 1 Tbsp (135g) boiling water

¼ cup (60 g) cold water

4 tsp (20g) neutral oil, plus more for rolling

Roux

2 Tbsp (28g) neutral oil

½ cup (60g) all-purpose flour

-

¼ cup (about 40g) raw white sesame seeds

(continued)

3 To make the roux: In a small nonstick pan set over medium-low heat, add the oil and flour, stirring to combine. Cook for 6 to 8 minutes, until the color of the roux turns a darker shade and the fragrance of toasted flour fills the room. Transfer the roux to a small bowl and set it aside to cool.

4 Place the sesame seeds in a shallow bowl and set aside. Lightly oil the work surface. Turn the rested dough onto the work surface and roll it out into a 15 by 12-inch rectangular sheet, about ¼ inch thick. Using a pastry scraper, spread the roux on top, leaving a roughly ½-inch border. Starting from one long edge, roll the sheet up into a log. Pinch the ends shut.

5 Cut the log into four even-size pieces. Pinch all the cut sides shut to contain the roux. Take one piece of dough, sit it cut-side up, and press it down with your palm to flatten it into a disk. ❼ Roll the disk out with a rolling pin into a rectangular sheet about 8 inches long and about ¼ inch thick. ❽ Fold the top quarter down to the center of the rectangle and the bottom a little more than a quarter up, so it just overlaps the top fold. Press on the overlapped edges to secure them. ❾ Turn the dough 90 degrees and repeat the fold and press step. Dip the flat, no-seam side in the sesame seeds. Set it aside and repeat with the remaining three dough pieces. Cover them with a damp cloth so they don't dry out.

6 Line a pizza peel with a piece of parchment paper. Place the first portion of dough you shaped on the work surface, sesame-side up. Roll it out into a 7 by 4-inch rectangular sheet, ¼ inch thick, and transfer it to the prepared pizza peel. Repeat with the remaining three pieces of dough, working in the order you shaped them. Slide the parchment paper (with the pieces of dough on it) onto the preheated pizza stone. Bake for 6 to 8 minutes, until they are puffed with brown spots.

7 Let the shāobǐng cool slightly, then use scissors to cut open both short ends and one of the long ends so you can easily add your desired fillings. Be careful of the hot steam escaping the layers. Serve warm with fried crullers (page 85) or other fillings of your choice sandwiched in between the layers.

油條 yóutiáo | 油炸粿 iû-tsia̍h-ké

Fried Crullers

With all the hot drinks in the breakfast lineup, you need a good vehicle for dipping. There's nothing better than yóutiáo—hollow, crunchy sticks of fried dough. These stacked batons are each leavened with baking powder, which, upon contact with heat, releases gases and causes the dough to puff up in the most delectable way. Freeze any leftovers; they keep well for a few months in the freezer. Reheat in a 355°F (180°C) oven for a few minutes before serving.

Makes 4 crullers

2 cups (240g) all-purpose flour, plus more for dusting

1½ tsp (6g) baking powder

½ tsp (2g) baking soda

½ tsp salt

2 tsp (9g) neutral oil

1 cup plus 1 Tbsp (135g) cold water

4 cups neutral oil, for frying

Soy Milk 豆漿 (page 74), Peanut Rice Milk 米漿 (page 78), or Almond Tea 杏仁茶 (page 79), for dipping

1 In a large bowl, combine the flour, baking powder, baking soda, and salt. Stream in the neutral oil, mixing with chopsticks to incorporate, and add the cold water. (It's important to use cold water and not room-temperature water; you don't want the baking powder to react prematurely.) Mix and knead the dough in the bowl until just combined, soft but not sticky, rough, and dotted with bits of flour, 2 to 3 minutes. Cover with a damp towel and rest for 20 to 30 minutes to begin the gluten development. Knead the dough in the bowl again until smooth, about 1 minute. Cover and let the dough rest again to allow the gluten to fully relax, at least 2 hours more. (For better flavor and texture, I recommend making this dough the night before and letting it rest in the refrigerator overnight. The next day, let it come back to room temperature before continuing to work with it, about 1 hour.)

2 Over a generously floured work surface and with floured hands, gently pick up the dough, hold it on both ends, and stretch it out into a long oval strip about 13½ inches long and ¼ inch thick. If you meet resistance, lay the dough on the work surface and roll it out to a 13-inch length. (If the dough feels stiff and inelastic, the gluten has not rested sufficiently. Cover the dough with a cloth and let rest for 10 minutes before trying again.) Trim ½ inch off each end so the resulting dough is now a 12½-inch-long rectangular sheet. Flour a sharp knife and cut the sheet into eight even pieces. Pick up each piece and dip all the cut sides

(continued)

Fried Crullers —— continued

in flour—the flour prevents the cut sides from sticking together and closing up when you eventually stack the pieces.

3   In a wok over medium-high heat, warm 4 cups of neutral oil, until it reaches 365°F (185°C).

4   Using a pastry brush, brush off all the excess flour on the side facing up on each piece to create a flour-free surface. Fill a cup with water, dip a chopstick in it, and draw a line of water right down the center of four of the eight pieces. Stack the non-watered pieces, non-dusted surface down, on top of the watered pieces. Dry the chopstick, dust it with flour, and press it down lengthwise across the center of each stack to bind the two pieces together. Press down with ample force but not so much that the stack splits in half. Dust the finished pieces with extra flour so they don't dry out, and cover with a towel.

5   Once the oil reaches 365°F (185°C), lower the heat to medium or medium-low to keep the temperature constant. Working with one at a time, pick up the dough by its two ends and gently stretch it out to about 1½ times its original length. Lower the dough middle first into the oil, forming a U shape, and hold it there for 3 seconds before swiftly and carefully letting the ends leave your fingers. Turn the heat up to medium or medium-high to offset the drop in temperature when the dough enters. At the correct temperature, the dough should sink and stay beneath the oil for 3 to 5 seconds before floating up. As soon as the dough floats, use a pair of long chopsticks or tongs to flip the yóutiáo gently and swiftly over and over. Flip continuously for the next 30 seconds, until the dough visibly expands to two or three times its original size. Once the yóutiáo stops expanding, flip it once every 45 to 60 seconds until golden on all sides.

6   Transfer the yóutiáo onto a wire rack to drain and repeat with the remaining yóutiáo. This yóutiáo will be crisp yet soft and chewy. If you prefer a crispier yóutiáo, do a second fry. Heat the oil to 390°F (200°C) and fry the yóutiáo, all at once, for 10 to 15 seconds on each side, until golden brown. Transfer to a wire rack to drain.

7   Serve warm with your choice of hot drink for dipping.

飯糰 fàntuán | 飯丸 pn̄g-uân
Sticky Rice Roll

This plump oval sticky rice roll takes breakfast-on-the-go to flavorful, complex heights. You can swap out ingredients for whatever you like. Anything crunchy will provide textural contrast, and any preserved vegetables will supply salt and flavor. Filling and wrapping the fàntuán requires a little finesse: You want a nice balance between the amount of rice and salty ingredients; otherwise it may become too salty. Try to pack everything together tightly to create a firm chew. I tend to mix glutinous rice with purple rice, which brings an extra layer of flavor and is also easier on the stomach.

Note: Steaming the sticky rice with a bamboo steamer yields chewier, more distinct grains. You can also use a rice cooker with a 1:0.7 rice-to-water ratio, plus a small drizzle of neutral oil.

1 In a medium bowl, rinse and drain the sticky rice and purple rice three to five times, until the water is no longer murky. Cover the rice with water by about 2 inches. Soak for at least 4 hours or up to overnight.

2 In another medium bowl, soak the preserved mustard in water for about 30 minutes, until barely salty. (Different brands differ in saltiness, so timing will vary. Taste your preserved mustards to check on the timing required.) After soaking, drain and squeeze out any excess moisture. Set aside.

3 Line your bamboo steamer with a cheesecloth. Drain the rice and spread it out over the cloth-lined steamer. Use your fingertips to make holes throughout the sticky rice so that you can see the cloth on the bottom. (This also allows for better heat circulation.) Cover the rice with another cloth, then secure the lid. Set the steamer over boiling water on high heat and steam for 30 minutes. Splash some room-temperature water on the sticky rice to keep it moist and then continue to steam for 5 to

(continued)

Makes 3 sticky rice rolls

1 cup (220g) sticky, glutinous rice, preferably long-grain 長糯米

½ cup (100g) purple rice 紫米 (not the sticky variety) or any regular white rice

3½ oz (100g) preserved mustard 榨菜 or more fermented mustard greens

3½ oz (100g) Fermented Mustard Greens 酸菜 (page 35), preferably the core/stem portion

3½ oz (100g) Preserved Radish 菜脯 (page 42), chopped into ¼-inch mince

2 Tbsp neutral oil

2 tsp golden granulated sugar

½ tsp sesame oil 香油

¼ tsp black pepper, plus more as needed

3 (4-inch) pieces Fried Cruller 油條 (page 85) or use store-bought

Peanut Sugar (page 104) or vegetarian meat floss 素肉鬆

Sticky Rice Roll —— continued

10 minutes more, until the grains are very soft and tender. The rice should be a little softer than you want, as it will harden slightly when it cools down to eating temperature. Remove from the heat and set it aside, still covered, to keep it warm.

4 Gently rinse the fermented mustard greens to mellow the excess salt. Chop against the grain of the fibers into ¼-inch-thick strips.

5 In a wok over medium heat, stir-fry the preserved radish for 1 to 2 minutes, until the steam dissipates and the radishes smell fragrant. Transfer the radishes to a medium bowl and set aside. Rinse the wok and set it back over medium heat until just smoking. Add the fermented mustard greens and stir-fry for 1 to 2 minutes to steam off some moisture. Transfer the fermented greens to a small bowl and set aside. Repeat this stir-frying process once more with the preserved mustard.

6 Rinse the wok and set it back over medium heat one last time. Warm the neutral oil and add the mustard greens, preserved mustard, and sugar. Stir-fry for 1 to 2 minutes, until the greens are fragrant and crunchy. Add the sesame oil and black pepper, stirring to coat the greens and preserved mustard. Taste and adjust the seasoning. Transfer both to the bowl with the radishes and set aside.

7 Preheat the oven to 355°F (180°C). Place the crullers on a baking tray and bake for 6 to 8 minutes (or 10 to 12 minutes from frozen), until dark brown and very crunchy. Set aside.

8 Line a kitchen towel (12 by 12 inches is a good size) with a piece of plastic wrap. Spread the steamed rice into a 7 by 5-inch rectangle, ¼ to ½ inch thick, on the plastic wrap. Top with a layer of peanut sugar, then with a layer of the mustard greens, preserved greens, and radishes. Place the fried cruller at the top center of the pile.

9 Bring in all sides and squeeze tightly to wrap. There should be just enough rice, so the edges meet and close without overlapping. If the edges are not attaching well, fill the gaps with a little more rice. Unstick the plastic wrap from the towel and use it to wrap around the sticky rice roll. Serve warm.

香椿抓餅 xiāngchūn zhuābǐng

Flaky Toon Pancakes

Chinese Toon (*Toona sinensis*) is often equated with scallions among Taiwanese Buddhist vegetarians, who abstain from consuming alliums. Some people compare it to the flavor of beef, though to me it is more like a gamy onion. Toon is something that took me a while to get used to, as it is never present in nonvegetarian Taiwanese food. I grew a taste for it, however, when the nuns introduced me to this flaky pancake. Now I sometimes make the toon sauce by itself and use it to flavor my fried rice and noodles.

Note: You can make these pancakes ahead of time and freeze them for up to 1 month. After you've flattened the pancakes into disks, stack them one on top of another, with parchment paper in between each piece. Freeze them on a plate or tray until solid, then pack them into freezer-safe bags. They can be fried from frozen; just add about 1 minute to the frying time.

1 To make the toon sauce: Remove the stalks and central stems from all the toon leaves. Wash the leaves and pat them dry. Transfer to a bamboo drying basket or steel tray and set in the sun or air-dry in a cool place until just dry to the touch, 1 to 2 hours. In a blender, combine the leaves and reddish buds, neutral oil, and salt and blend until an oily, fine paste that looks like pesto forms. Set aside.

2 In a large mixing bowl, combine 2 cups of the flour and the salt. Add the water and mix with a pair of chopsticks until a dough just comes together, 2 to 3 minutes. The dough should feel very sticky and difficult to work with; the high hydration is what will result in a soft, tender interior. Cover with a damp towel and let rest for 20 minutes to begin the gluten development. Knead the dough until smooth, 1 to 2 minutes more. Cover and let rest for at least another 2 hours and preferably overnight.

Makes 3 pancakes

Toon Sauce

1 oz (30g) Chinese Toon (*Toona sinensis*) 香椿, reddish buds and green leaves

¼ cup neutral oil

Pinch of salt

-

2 cups (240g) plus 2 Tbsp (15 g) all-purpose flour

½ tsp salt

⅔ cup (160g) water

Neutral oil

Pepper Salt 胡椒鹽 (page 113)

(continued)

Flaky Toon Pancakes ——— continued

3 In a small mixing bowl, combine the remaining 2 Tbsp flour and the toon sauce to make a roux. Mix until smooth and no lumps remain, then set aside.

4 Oil the work surface, the rolling pin, and your hands. Divide the dough evenly into three portions, about 130g each. Roll each portion into a ball and cover them loosely with a damp cloth. Roll out the first dough ball you shaped as thinly as possible into a rectangular sheet about 1/16 inch thick.

5 Brush on a thin layer of the roux (about 2 Tbsp), leaving a clean 1/2- to 3/4-inch outer border on all sides. Sprinkle on the pepper salt to taste. Starting from the bottom-left corner of one of the long sides, fold the dough in 2-inch increments toward the upper-right corner, repeating a pull-fold-pull-fold motion, and pressing each fold to squeeze out any trapped air. Once you get to the top and have a long rectangular baton, flatten it slightly and fold it lengthwise. Begin coiling the dough by taking one end and circling it once over. This will be the center top of the coiled pancake. Continue to coil under, creating about three layers of stacked coils, and secure the very end at the center bottom of the coil. Place the coiled dough back under the cloth. Repeat with the remaining two dough balls. Once all are coiled, let rest for at least another 10 minutes and up to 2 hours.

6 Using a rolling pin, flatten the pancakes into 8-inch disks, about 1/4 inch thick. In a flat cast-iron or nonstick pan, warm 1 Tbsp neutral oil over high heat. Fry the pancake for 1 to 2 minutes, until golden underneath, and flip to fry the other side, 1 to 2 minutes more. When nearly done, you should see the pancake start to puff up slightly. Holding a spatula in one hand and tongs in the other, shove the pancake on its bottom edge. It should rotate by itself along that edge. Shove the pancake just enough so that all of the layers release but remain intact, like a bloomed rose.

7 Once both sides are golden brown and crisp, transfer to a wire rack to cool. Sprinkle some pepper salt on top and serve immediately.

麻醬麵 májiàngmiàn
Sesame Noodles

These thin strands of noodles are mixed with a nutty, shallot-heavy, sweet, and slightly tangy sauce. It's the noodles that I always ate as a kid when I stayed home on a typhoon day and didn't know what to eat. A spoonful of chili oil is a must, and mine is a special one, not very spicy but distinctly fragrant and tingly. The chili and Sichuan pepper dance on the tongue, reminding us that oftentimes simple and wholesome food is all we really long for.

1 To make the sesame sauce: In a medium bowl, combine the sesame paste, peanut butter, and water. Once the pastes have loosened and smoothed out, add the light soy sauce, sugar, rice vinegar, sesame oil, salt, and fried shallots and mix well. Taste and adjust the seasoning with salt and/or sugar as needed and set aside.

2 Bring a large pot of water to a gentle boil. Cook the noodles according to the package directions, or to your desired doneness, and drain and transfer the noodles into serving bowls. Carry a bit of water with the noodles into the bowls; it helps keep the noodles moist and loosen the sesame sauce.

3 In the same pot of water, add a pinch of salt (this helps season and rid bitterness in the vegetables that will follow). Add the stem portions of the bok choy first, wait 10 seconds, then add the greens along with the bean sprouts. Blanch for another 15 seconds, until the greens are vibrantly colored and the bean sprouts are just wilted but still crunchy. Using a spider strainer, remove the vegetables and add them to the bowls with the noodles.

4 Top each bowl with the sesame sauce, chili oil, and scallions. Mix while still hot and serve immediately.

Serves 4

Sesame Sauce

¼ cup (70g) sesame paste

¼ cup (70g) peanut butter

⅔ cup water

2 Tbsp light soy sauce

2 Tbsp golden granulated sugar, plus more as needed

2 tsp rice vinegar

2 tsp sesame oil 香油

½ tsp salt, plus more as needed

¼ cup (60g) Fried Shallots 油蔥 (page 175)

-

4 portions plain wheat noodles 陽春麵 or noodles of your choice (600g fresh / 300g dried)

Pinch of salt

2 heads white-stemmed bok choy or vegetables of choice (100g), cut into 1½- to 2-inch segments, stems and greens separated

7 oz (200g) mung bean sprouts

Chili Oil (recipe follows) and chopped scallions (both white and green parts), for serving

(continued)

辣油 làyóu

Chili Oil

1 In a saucepan over medium-low heat, combine the neutral oil, ginger, and garlic (if using). Cook and slowly bring the oil temperature up to 350° to 360°F (176° to 182°C), 10 to 15 minutes.

2 Meanwhile, in the bowl of a spice grinder, grind the Sichuan peppercorns and dried chilies into a fine powder. Transfer the mixture to a heatproof bowl, along with the chili flakes, star anise, toasted sesame seeds, light soy sauce, salt, and MSG (if using). Roughly mix everything together.

3 When the garlic and ginger are golden brown, remove and discard them. Swiftly and carefully, pour half of the oil over the chili mixture in the heatproof bowl. The chili flakes should sizzle and bubble rapidly (rising almost like foam) as soon as the hot oil hits them. Stir the mixture around to evenly distribute the heat and oil, then add the remaining hot oil, stirring again. The chilies should continue to sizzle for a couple more seconds after adding all the oil and give off a toasty, caramel fragrance that doesn't smell burnt. Set the bowl aside to let it cool completely.

4 Once cooled, pour the chili oil (and all the sediment) into a lidded 1-cup glass container. Refrigerate overnight before using; the flavors need time to meld together. Store in the refrigerator for up to 6 months.

Makes one 1-cup jar

1 cup neutral oil

1 (1-inch) piece peeled ginger, sliced

2 garlic cloves, lightly crushed (optional)

2 Tbsp (8g) red Sichuan peppercorns 大紅砲

½ cup (10g) dried red chilies, preferably cháotiānjiāo chilies 朝天椒

½ cup (50g) coarse red chili flakes, preferably èrjīngtiáo chili flakes 二荆條粗粉

1 whole star anise pod (1g)

2 Tbsp (15g) toasted white sesame seeds

2 tsp light soy sauce

¼ tsp salt

Pinch of MSG (optional)

Little Eats

"Little eats" is my direct translation of the term xiǎochī (小吃), which is street food that carries the tradition of dim sum—small bites and big flavors. Taiwan's street food scene is iconic—the viral videos of vendors cutting into steaming-hot, jiggly castella cakes and of cooks flipping rippling bodies of fried rice on woks with flames searingly high have reached audiences far and wide. The culture and food of this island have a life of their own.

These days, the dishes representative of eating out sometimes remind me of home more than home cooking does. They take me back to the after-school strolls with my friends under the hazy skirts of Taipei streetlights. Grease-stained bag of popcorn chicken in one hand, a cool drink in the other, and conversations that never end. Ah, what was it like to be carefree and happy with very little?

酥炸豆包 sūzhà dòubāo

Crispy Fried Tofu Skin

Serves 4 to 6 as part of a spread

Garlic Soy Paste
蒜蓉油膏

3 or 4 garlic cloves or pickled garlic (page 18), finely minced

2 Tbsp soy sauce paste

½ tsp golden granulated sugar, plus more as needed

-

2 cups neutral oil, for frying

14 oz (400g) whole fresh tofu skin rolls 豆包

Pinch of Pepper Salt 胡椒鹽 (page 113)

Pickled Cabbage 台式泡菜 (recipe follows), for serving

The nuns always speak about tofu skin like it is a kind of blessing, and rightfully so, because it is delicious and has more protein per gram than chicken breast. These tofu skin rolls are fried until shatteringly crisp on the outside, while remaining soft and tender on the inside. If you see different kinds of tofu skin rolls at the market, look for ones that feel moist and bouncy. Firmer ones are good for braising but can be slightly dry when fried. Táishì pàocài (Taiwanese-style pickled cabbage, page 103), which you'll need to make a day in advance, is typically served alongside a fried dish like this to cut through the richness. Sometimes I throw a few suānméi (dried plums) or fresh pineapple trimmings, skins and core, into the pickle to bring an extra source of fruity sourness.

1 To make the garlic soy paste: In a small dish, mix the minced garlic, soy sauce paste, and sugar. Taste and adjust the sweetness with sugar as needed. Set aside.

2 In a wok over high heat, warm the neutral oil until it reaches 355°F (180°C). Make sure the oil comes up to this temperature; otherwise the tofu skin will not keep its shape. Slide in three or four tofu skin rolls one by one; try not to overcrowd the wok as the rolls can stick together. Fry for about 1 minute on each side, until evenly puffed and lightly golden. Using a spider strainer or slotted spoon, transfer to a paper towel–lined plate and set aside to drain.

3 Line a plate with paper towels. Reheat the oil back up to 355°F (180°C) and fry all of the tofu skin rolls once more for 3 to 5 seconds, until crispy and golden. Remove and drain on the prepared plate. Dash lightly with the pepper salt.

4 Chop each roll into four squares and transfer them to a serving plate. Serve immediately, with the garlic soy paste and pickled cabbage on the side.

(continued)

台式泡菜 táishì pàocài

Pickled Cabbage

1 Remove the green cabbage's outer leaves and cut out the core; the trimmed cabbage should weigh about 900g. Compost or save the cabbage outer leaves and core for stock. Tear the inner leaves by hand into 2- to 3-inch pieces and tear the thicker stems into 1- to 1½-inch pieces. In a large bowl, combine the torn cabbage and carrot. Massage all the pieces with the salt for 1 minute or so, to evenly distribute the salt, and set aside for 1 hour, until they've reduced in volume by half and are limp and slightly translucent.

2 In a medium pot over high heat, bring the rice vinegar, mirin, and sugar to a boil, stirring constantly. Boil until the sugar is just fully dissolved, 30 to 60 seconds. Set this pickling liquid aside to cool completely.

3 Drain and discard the liquid from the cabbage and carrots. Add the garlic, ginger, red chilies, and the cooled pickling liquid and toss to combine. Pack the cabbage mixture tightly into a lidded 4-cup glass container. The pieces should all be fully submerged in the liquid. Secure the lid and let ferment in the refrigerator for at least 1 day before enjoying. Store in the refrigerator for up to 10 days.

Makes one 4-cup jar

One head green cabbage (1,200g)

½ peeled carrot (100g), cut into thin batons

1½ Tbsp (27g) salt

¾ cup rice vinegar

¼ cup mirin 味霖

¾ cup (150g) white rock sugar

6 garlic cloves, lightly crushed

1 (1-inch) piece peeled ginger (10g), julienned

2 fresh red chilies, sliced into ¾-inch segments on a bias

割包 guàbāo | kuah-pau

Gua Bao

Guàbāo has two nicknames: "Taiwanese hamburger" and hǔyǎozhū (虎咬豬), meaning "tiger biting a pig," for the way the steamed bun closes its mouth shut with the porky filling inside. It's phonemically similar to fúyǎozhù (福咬住), which means holding on to good fortune. Both names are fitting—there is so much flavor packed into each mouthful that you'll wish you could savor it a little longer. Vegetarian street pushcarts swap out the pork for braised gluten, but the rest is the same: a pillowy, soft steamed bun with salty-sour mustard greens, peanut sugar, and cilantro. In place of star anise and cinnamon, you can try a different flavor by substituting 1 to 2 tsp of shísānxiāng (Thirteen-Spice, page 27).

1 **To make the bāo:** In a large bowl, combine the flour, baking powder, and sugar. In a small bowl, dissolve the instant yeast in the water. Add the yeast-water mixture to the dry ingredients and mix with chopsticks until you get something shaggy and light that resembles snowflakes. Add the neutral oil and, with your hands, mix in the oil and bring the dough together. Knead in the bowl until the dough is mostly smooth, no longer sticky, and no batter sticks to the sides of the bowl, 6 to 8 minutes. Oil the bowl lightly and place the dough back in it. Cover with a damp cloth and proof at room temperature for 1 to 2 hours, or until doubled in size.

2 **To make the peanut sugar:** Preheat the oven to 355°F (180°C). Spread the peanuts in a single layer on a baking tray. Roast for 12 to 15 minutes, stirring occasionally, until the peanuts are golden and smell nutty. Set aside to cool to room temperature. In a food processor, pulse the cooled peanuts and sugar until the mixture resembles a coarse powder. Set aside.

3 **To make the braised gluten:** Dig your thumb into the center top of each gluten intestine, then pry it open to reveal its layers. Tear it by hand

(continued)

Makes 6 baos

Bāo

1¾ cups (220g) all-purpose flour

1 tsp (4g) baking powder

1 Tbsp (15g) granulated sugar (any kind)

1 tsp (3g) instant yeast

½ cup (120g) water

1 Tbsp (14g) neutral oil, plus more for brushing

Peanut Sugar

½ cup (100g) unsalted raw, shelled peanuts

¼ cup (50g) golden granulated sugar

Braised Gluten

4 Gluten Intestines 麵腸 (page 58) or use store-bought (400g total)

¼ cup neutral oil

2 (1-inch) pieces ginger, sliced

2 scallions (40g), both white and green parts, cut into 1-inch segments

(continued)

Gua Bao —— continued

into irregularly shaped 1½- to 2-inch chunks. In a wok over medium to medium-high heat, warm the neutral oil. Swirl the oil around to create a nonstick surface and add the gluten chunks, constantly stirring until lightly golden throughout, 2 to 3 minutes. Add the ginger and scallions and stir-fry to release their fragrances, 30 to 60 seconds. Add the golden granulated sugar, star anise, and cinnamon stick and toss a few more times, taking care not to burn the spices. Swirl in the soy sauce and cooking wine and continue frying for 15 to 30 seconds, until the fragrance has deepened. Add the fried shallots and fermented bean curd, smushing the bean curd in to coat the wheat gluten pieces. Add the water and season with salt. Lower the heat to a slow boil and braise, uncovered, for 15 to 20 minutes, until the sauce has reduced almost entirely and the gluten chunks have softened but still have a chewy texture. Taste and adjust the seasoning as needed. Remove from the heat, cover the wok with a lid, and set aside.

4 Line a bamboo or steel steamer with parchment paper. Remove the proofed bāo dough from the oiled bowl onto a work surface and divide it into six equal-size portions, 61g to 62g each. Roll each portion into a smooth ball. Using one-way strokes with a rolling pin, roll out one ball into an oval about 6 inches long and 3 inches wide. Brush a very thin layer of neutral oil on the bottom half of the less smooth side of the dough; this will be the inside of the bāo. Working quickly, nestle the shaped guàbāo one by one into the bamboo steamer. Cover and proof for 30 minutes more, until they appear fuller, slightly puffed, and about 1½ times the original size.

5 Bring a large pot of water to a boil over high heat. Place the steamer over the boiling water and steam, with the heat still on high, for 12 minutes. Remove the pot from the heat and let it sit for 3 to 5 minutes before removing the lid of the steamer.

6 To fill the guàbāo: Assemble the guàbāo like a sandwich: stuff it with cilantro, braised gluten, mustard greens, and peanut sugar. Alternatively, serve all the components as a spread and let everyone assemble guàbāo to their own liking at the table.

2 tsp golden granulated sugar

3 whole (3g) star anise pods

1 (½-inch) piece cinnamon stick (1g)

2 Tbsp light soy sauce

2 Tbsp Taiwanese rice cooking wine

2 tsp (10g) Fried Shallots 油蔥 (page 175)

1 small cube (8g) Sweet Wine Fermented Bean Curd 豆腐乳 (page 52) or use store-bought

2 cups water

½ tsp salt

Filling

1 cup chopped cilantro leaves plus tender stems

Stir-Fried Mustard Greens 炒酸菜 (recipe follows)

炒酸菜 chǎosuāncài

Stir-Fried Mustard Greens

1 In a small bowl, soak the dried mushrooms in water to cover until fully soft, 20 to 30 minutes. Snip off and discard the stems, chop the caps into a rough mince, and set aside. Discard the soaking liquid.

2 Gently rinse the mustard greens to mellow the excess salt without ridding the greens of their prized flavor. Chop into a ¼-inch mince. The leaves can get tangled; chop them through a few more times so they won't be in long strands.

3 Warm a wok over medium heat until just smoking. Add the fermented mustard greens and fry for 1 to 2 minutes to allow some moisture to steam off. Transfer the greens to a bowl.

4 In the same wok over medium heat, warm the neutral oil until hot. Add the ginger and red chili and fry to release their fragrances, 15 to 30 seconds. Add the mushrooms and fry for 1 to 2 minutes to release their fragrance. Add the mustard greens, tossing to combine. Add the sugar, swirl in the sesame oil, and stir-fry for another 2 to 3 minutes, until the greens are fragrant and crunchy. Taste and adjust the seasoning as needed, adding more sugar if it is still too sour.

5 Serve warm as a side dish, sandwiched in between guàbāo (page 104), or on top of hóngshāomiàn (Beef Noodle Soup, page 161).

Serves 4 as a side

2 dried shiitake mushrooms (10g)

1 head Fermented Mustard Greens 酸菜 (page 35; 400g)

2 Tbsp neutral oil

2 tsp minced ginger

1 fresh red chili (10g), cut into thin rings

4 tsp golden granulated sugar, plus more as needed

1 tsp sesame oil 香油

蚵仔煎 ô-á-tsian

Oyster Omelet

The oyster omelet, in its original street-food form, is oysters, eggs, and greens glued together with a starch slurry and fried on a greased flattop. This vegetarian version makes use of mushrooms, tofu skin, and gluten to create something that is just as interesting and textured. The star of the show is the haishan sauce, a rice flour–thickened sauce known as mǐjiàng (米醬), the Taiwanese equivalent of a French "mother sauce." Each *ô-á-tsian* vendor has their own version; mine makes use of miso and my own fermented chili sauces. It is sweet, tart, umami, and spicy—a seriously irresistible combination.

1 To make the haishan sauce: In a small saucepan, combine the sugar, fermented chili paste, sweet chili sauce, soy sauce paste, rice cooking wine, and ½ cup of the water. In a small bowl, make a slurry with the rice flour and the remaining 2 Tbsp water. Set the saucepan over medium heat and bring it up to a slow boil. Once it's boiling, whisk in the miso until smooth. Bring the sauce to a gentle boil again and drizzle in the slurry, whisking constantly, until it reaches your desired thickness (you may not need all the slurry, but I tend to add it all). Taste and season with salt if needed. Set aside and cover to keep warm.

2 To make the omelet batter: In a large bowl, whisk together the water, sweet potato starch, tapioca starch, and garlic chives.

3 In another bowl, run the gluten puffs under warm water. They should almost instantly deflate and soften. Squeeze out the excess water.

4 In a small nonstick pan over medium heat, warm the neutral oil. Sauté the straw mushrooms for about 45 seconds, until they appear soft and smell fragrant. Add the tofu skin, gluten puffs, and salt and continue to sauté about 1 minute, until the tofu skin and gluten puffs are lightly browned and caramelized.

Serves 1

Haishan Sauce 海山醬 (makes ¾ cup)

1 Tbsp golden granulated sugar

1½ tsp Fermented Chili Paste 辣椒醬 (page 16)

2 Tbsp Sweet Chili Sauce 甜辣醬 (page 17)

1 Tbsp soy sauce paste

1 tsp Taiwanese rice cooking wine

½ cup plus 2 Tbsp water

1 Tbsp (10g) rice flour 在來米粉

1½ tsp (15g) light brown miso

Salt

Omelet Batter

¼ cup water

2 Tbsp (16g) sweet potato starch 地瓜粉

1 Tbsp (8g) tapioca starch 樹薯粉

1 garlic chive 韭菜, chopped

5 Stir the omelet batter once more to bring it together and ladle it into the pan, tilting it slightly until the batter evenly coats the bottom. Add the a-cài, sprinkle on the nori flakes (if using), and cook for 1 to 2 minutes, until the batter turns slightly translucent. Using a spatula, loosen the sides of the omelet, fold it in half, and flip the entire omelet over. The omelet won't be a perfect half-moon shape, and instead it will be a blob—a messy work of art, if you will. Fry the omelet for another 1 minute on the other side, then carefully transfer it to a plate. Spoon warm haishan sauce generously over the omelet and serve.

¾ cup (12g) Gluten Puffs 麵筋泡 (page 60) or more tofu skin rolls

1 Tbsp neutral oil

2 oz (60g) fresh or canned peeled straw mushrooms 草菇 or other fresh mushrooms, cut into 1-inch chunks

1 oz (30g) fresh tofu skin rolls 豆包, roughly torn into 1- to 2-inch pieces

⅛ tsp salt

About ¼ cup a-cài (Taiwanese lettuce) or other leafy greens chopped into 2-inch segments

Sprinkle of nori flakes (optional)

碗粿 uánn-kué

Bowl Rice Cake

Uánn-kué translates literally to "bowl rice cake." My A-Má makes it frequently at home, because "it's easy." There are no steps required to make sure the shape is perfect, and you can eat it straight from the bowl it's cooked in. She—and many street stalls in southern Taiwan—mixes a few spoons of braised pork broth into the rice slurry, which results in a brown cake. I wanted this to be a simpler recipe and one that emphasizes the flavor of the rice, so I kept mine white and added some fried shallots.

From making it so many times, A-Má learned that the rice cake cooked quicker when she used boiling water to scald the slurry. This step is integral to a successful *uánn-kué*, as the rice particles become less likely to sediment and separate during the steaming process. When the ingredients and technique are proper, you'll find that the sides rise and the middle sinks a little. For most *uánn-kué* connoisseurs, the little dip is an indication of quality. Be sure to let the *uánn-kué* cool to room temperature before enjoying. That's how they get their chewy, springy "Q" texture!

1 In a medium bowl, rinse and drain the rice three to five times, until the water runs mostly clear. Soak the washed rice in ⅔ cup of the water for 2 to 4 hours, until the grains are translucent throughout and easily split when pinched.

2 In a small bowl, soak the dried shiitake mushrooms with enough warm water to cover for 30 minutes, or until just fully soft. Remove the mushrooms, set them aside, and reserve the soaking liquid in the bowl.

3 In a blender, blend the rice and all of its soaking liquid on high speed for 2 to 4 minutes, until you get a smooth rice slurry without any graininess. Add the sweet potato starch and salt and pulse a few more times to incorporate. Transfer the slurry to a large heatproof bowl.

(continued)

Makes 3 bowls

⅓ cup plus 1 Tbsp (100g) aged Taiwanese chailai indica rice 在來米 or aged basmati rice

1⅔ cups water

8 mini dried shiitake mushrooms (12 g)

2 Tbsp (16g) fine sweet potato starch

¼ tsp salt

2 tsp (10g) Fried Shallots 油蔥 (page 175) or use store-bought

2 Tbsp neutral oil

3 oz (90g) Preserved Radish 菜脯 (page 42), cut into ¼-inch mince

Sweet Soy Sauce Paste

2½ Tbsp light soy sauce

1½ Tbsp golden granulated sugar

1½ cups plus 2 Tbsp water

3 pieces gan cao (dried licorice root) 甘草

1 Tbsp (8g) fine sweet potato starch

Salt

-

Pureed raw garlic

Bowl Rice Cake —— continued

4 In a small saucepan over high heat, bring the remaining 1 cup water to a rolling boil. Pour the hot water all at once (but carefully), and from a high vantage point, into the rice slurry bowl while vigorously stirring in one direction until fully incorporated, about 1 minute. Mix in the fried shallots and set aside.

5 Set a wok over high heat and heat it until it just starts smoking. Ladle in the neutral oil, swirl it around to create a nonstick surface, and pour out the oil, reserving it on the side. Add the minced preserved radish and stir-fry for 1 to 2 minutes, until the steam dissipates and the radish smells fragrant. Transfer the radish to a bowl and set aside. To the wok, add 1 tsp of the reserved neutral oil and the shiitake mushrooms and stir-fry 1 to 2 minutes, until fragrant. Add a splash of the mushroom soaking liquid and continue to fry until dry. Transfer the mushrooms to a bowl and set aside.

6 To make the sweet soy sauce paste: In a small saucepan, combine the light soy sauce, sugar, 1½ cups of the water, and the gan cao. Bring to a gentle boil over medium-high heat, then lower the heat so it is barely bubbling. Cook uncovered for 5 minutes. Meanwhile, in a separate bowl, make a slurry with the sweet potato starch and the remaining 2 Tbsp water. Drizzle the slurry into the sauce, stirring constantly to incorporate. Once the sauce has thickened, remove it from the heat and set aside to cool. Season with salt to taste.

7 Set a bamboo or steel steamer over boiling water and nestle in three upside-down rice bowls. Cover with the lid and steam on high for about 3 minutes to preheat the bowls. Wearing heatproof gloves, carefully flip the bowls over and swiftly ladle in the rice slurry, dividing it evenly among the three bowls. Steam for 10 minutes and then place 2 shiitake mushrooms at or near the center of each bowl. Cover and continue steaming for another 10 to 15 minutes, until no liquid slurry remains and the rice pudding appears shiny and a little translucent throughout.

8 Remove the bowls from the steamer (be careful, they're hot) and set them aside to cool completely. Top with the sweet soy sauce paste, preserved radish, and pureed garlic and serve.

鹹酥菇 xiánsūgū | kiâm-soo-koo

Popcorn Mushrooms

Many people strolling around a night market are lured in by vendors selling some form of fried "popcorn" food. These mushrooms are fried with a tempura-like batter that makes their outsides light and airy while their insides are bursting with juiciness. Complement the mushrooms with an array of other fried goods: corn, beans, rice cakes, or potatoes. To make sure everything is perfectly crisp, mimic the way a street vendor does it. Fry everything up to 1 hour before serving, and right before you're ready to eat, fry it once more.

Serves 4 to 6

1 To make the pepper salt: In a small dish, mix together the salt, white pepper, black pepper, ground Sichuan pepper, five-spice, and MSG (if using) and set aside.

2 To make the batter: In a medium bowl, sift the cake flour and baking powder. Add the water and, using a chopstick, mix just until a batter forms. Be careful not to overmix and subsequently develop gluten. The batter doesn't have to be silky smooth and can have some lumps.

3 Prepare your station for the first fry. Set the batter close to the stove. Add the cornstarch to a large bowl. Set a cooling rack over a baking tray. In a wok over medium-high heat, warm the neutral oil until it reaches 340° to 355°F (170° to 180°C).

4 For the mushrooms, baby corn, and green beans, fry one ingredient at a time and maintain the oil at 340° to 355°F (170° to 180°C). Coat the ingredients lightly with cornstarch, shake off the excess, and coat lightly with the batter. Drop them one by one in the hot oil. Fry until lightly golden, 1½ to 3 minutes per ingredient. Set them on the cooling rack to drain.

5 Coat the purple laver cake pieces lightly with cornstarch. Fry at 340°F (170°C) for 2 to 3 minutes, until a crisp, white shell develops on the outside. Set on the cooling rack to drain.

(continued)

Pepper Salt 胡椒鹽

1 tsp salt

¾ tsp white pepper

¼ tsp black pepper

⅛ tsp ground Sichuan pepper

⅛ tsp Five-Spice (page 27)

Pinch of MSG (optional)

Batter

1 cup (120g) cake flour

½ tsp baking powder

¾ cup (180g) cold water

-

½ cup (60g) cornstarch, plus more as needed, for dusting

3 cups neutral oil, for frying

1 large cluster (100g) oyster mushrooms, trimmed and torn into individual buds, or enoki mushrooms, torn into smaller bundles

(continued)

6   Coat the sweet potato batons lightly with cornstarch. Lower the heat to 320°F (160°C) and fry for 3 to 5 minutes, until vibrantly orange.

7   When ready to serve, reheat the oil to 355°F (180°C). Fry each ingredient once more, for 10 to 30 seconds each, until golden, lightly browned, and crisp. Transfer to the wire rack and immediately sprinkle the pepper salt on the mushrooms, baby corn, green beans, and purple laver cake and the plum powder (if using) on the sweet potatoes.

8   Slightly lower the heat and cool the oil to 320°F (160°C). Using the wok's lid as a shield, drop the basil leaves in and fry for about 10 seconds, until vibrantly green. Using a spider strainer or slotted spoon, carefully transfer the basil leaves to a serving platter so as not to shatter the now crisp and brittle leaves. Season with the pepper salt. Serve immediately with the rest of the fried goods.

3½ oz (100g) fresh shiitake mushrooms, stems removed, kept whole or halved at an angle if large

3½ oz (100g) baby corn 玉米筍, husked and kept whole

3½ oz (100g) green beans 菜豆/四季豆, ends trimmed and halved, or cauliflower or broccoli, torn into florets

7 oz (200g) Purple Laver Cake 紫菜糕 (recipe follows) or Turnip Cake 蘿蔔糕 (page 234)

7 oz (200g) orange-fleshed sweet potatoes or russet potatoes, peeled, cut into ½-inch-thick batons, and soaked in water until ready to fry

Taiwanese plum powder 梅粉 (optional)

1 bunch (20g to 25g) Taiwanese basil leaves 九層塔 or Thai basil leaves

紫菜糕 zǐcàigāo | 智慧糕 tì-huī-kué

Purple Laver Cake

This is a traditional vegetarian version of pig's blood cake (in Taiwanese, *tì-hueh-kué*). It is commonly referred to as "wisdom cake," since "wisdom" (in Taiwanese, *tì-huī*) is phonetically similar to "pig's blood." But rather than blood, this cake uses the thickening power of a rice slurry, which yields a nearly equivalent springy and chewy texture.

1 In a large bowl, rinse and drain 1 cup of the long-grain sticky rice three to five times, until the water runs mostly clear. Soak the washed rice with enough water to cover by at least 1 inch. In a separate medium bowl, combine the remaining ¼ cup long-grain sticky rice and the purple rice. Rinse and drain, place in a bowl, and add the 1¼ cups of water. Let both bowls of rice soak at room temperature for at least 8 hours or overnight.

2 Line an 8 by 6-inch pan with parchment paper. Drain only the sticky rice and set it aside. In a blender, combine the contents of the second bowl (sticky rice, purple rice, and water), the purple laver, salt, white pepper, mushroom powder (if using), and sesame oil and blend on high until a very smooth and fine paste forms, 3 to 4 minutes. Pour the paste into the bowl with the sticky rice. Mix thoroughly, transfer it into the prepared pan, and smooth the top. The mixture should be about 1 inch tall. Steam, uncovered, over medium-high heat, for 30 minutes, until a chopstick inserted in the center comes out mostly clean.

3 Keep the cake in the pan and let it cool to room temperature. Cover and transfer the cake to the refrigerator for at least 2 hours and preferably overnight, until slightly hardened. Using an oiled knife, loosen the cake's edges and carefully turn it out of the pan. Cut lengthwise into ¾- to 1-inch slices, then cut each slice in half crosswise. If you're not eating this the same day, pack it into an airtight freezable container and freeze for up to 2 months. Thaw completely before using.

Makes 16 pieces

1 cup (220g) plus ¼ cup (55g) long-grain sticky/glutinous rice 長糯米

¼ cup (50g) purple rice 紫米 (not the sticky variety)

1¼ cups water

1 bundle (about 20g) purple laver 紫菜 or nori (seaweed) sheets

½ tsp salt

¼ tsp white pepper

½ tsp Mushroom Powder 香菇粉 (page 15) or store-bought (optional)

2 tsp sesame oil 香油

滷味 lǔwèi

Soy-Braised Goods

My trips to the Daxi District in Taoyuan City inspired me to delve deeper into the craft of soy braising. Daxi is one of the most, if not *the* most, esteemed districts for soy products; on the old street, the scents of caramel and anise perfume everywhere. It was no surprise to see all kinds of plump-looking tofu, bean curd, and soy chickens floating atop the dark, glistening braising stocks. Vendors fish out what you want, slice them, and serve them on a platter just like this recipe. When done right, Taiwanese lǔwèi is gently sweet, not too salty, and has a balanced spice profile.

1 To make the braising stock: In a large pot, soak the kombu and dried shiitake mushrooms in the water for 1 to 1½ hours, until the mushrooms are soft and the kombu is smooth and full. Transfer the mushrooms, kombu, and broth to separate bowls and set aside.

2 In a large pot over medium-high heat, warm the neutral oil until hot. Add the ginger, garlic, scallions, and dried red chilies and sauté for 1 minute, until fragrant and blistered. Add the rock sugar and fry until it melts and turns an amber color. Stir in both the black and white peppercorns, the light soy sauce, and black vinegar, continuously stirring to ensure all the sugar has dissolved. Cook for about 1 minute, until very fragrant. Increase the heat to high, add the rice cooking wine and kombu-mushroom broth, bring to a rolling boil, then lower the heat so the liquid is still bubbling but not as rapidly. Stir in the maltose syrup (if using), taking care nothing sticks to the bottom, and add the braising pouch. Cover partially and cook for 1 hour, until the broth has reduced by about one-third of its original amount. Taste for seasoning and dilute with more water or reduce further as desired.

3 To begin braising, take note of how much braising stock you have. In general, the stock can braise an equal weight of food before it begins to lose its flavor and potency. Pour out the amount of stock you need and freeze the rest for up to 3 months.

(continued)

Serves 8 to 10 as part of a spread

Braising Stock 滷汁 (makes 10½ to 12 cups / 2,500 to 2,800ml)

8 (5-inch) pieces kombu 海帶 (35g)

8 dried shiitake mushrooms (20g)

12½ cups water, plus more as needed

3 Tbsp neutral oil

1 (3-inch) piece ginger (50g), unpeeled and sliced

12 garlic cloves (40g), lightly crushed

2 scallions (40g), both green and white parts, cut into 1-inch segments

6 dried red chilies, seeded and cut into ½-inch segments

1 cup (200g) yellow rock sugar

1 Tbsp (10g) black peppercorns

1 Tbsp (10g) white peppercorns

1½ cups light soy sauce

(continued)

Soy-Braised Goods —— continued

4 For flavors to fully permeate the ingredients, or to be rùwèi (入味), without breaking down or losing their desired texture, they need to be soaked in addition to braising. Braise each ingredient (see specific instructions below) at a slow boil or a simmer. Braise everything first, let the stock cool, and then soak everything together.

Bean curd or tofu: Fill a medium pot with 6¼ cups water and 1 tsp salt. Bring to a rolling boil over high heat, then lower to a gentle one. Blanch the bean curd for 3 minutes, remove, and drain. Braise the bean curd in the stock for 20 to 25 minutes and soak for at least 8 hours and up to 1 day.

Gluten intestine: In a wok over medium-high heat, warm 2 to 3 Tbsp neutral oil until hot. Shallow-fry the gluten intestines for 1 to 2 minutes on each side, until golden brown and puffed. Braise for 10 minutes and then soak for about 1 hour.

Soy chicken: Braise for 20 to 25 minutes and soak for at least 8 hours and up to 1 day.

King oyster and shiitake mushrooms: Braise for 20 to 25 minutes and soak for at least 1 hour and up to 1 day.

Tofu skin rolls: In a wok over medium-high heat, warm 2 to 3 Tbsp neutral oil until hot. Shallow-fry the tofu skin rolls for about 1 minute on each side, until golden and puffed. Braise for 5 to 10 minutes, depending on thickness; no need to soak.

Kombu rolls: Starting from the short side, roll up each piece of the reserved kombu by making four 1-inch folds. To secure the roll, pierce a toothpick at a point on the seam side about one-third from the bottom through one layer of kombu below it and pierce it back out from a point about one-third from the top. Braise for 5 to 10 minutes, until tender with a slight bite; no need to soak.

5 Slice all the braised goods into bite-size pieces. Drizzle or brush them with sesame oil and garnish with chopped cilantro, scallions, and/or red chiles. Serve warm, cold, or at room temperature, with chili oil or sweet chili sauce on the side for dipping.

¼ cup Taiwanese black vinegar 烏醋, preferably a Taiwanese-brand mild black vinegar with 1.8 percent acidity

1½ cups Taiwanese rice cooking wine

2 Tbsp (about 40g) maltose syrup 麥芽糖 (optional)

1 braising pouch with Thirteen-Spice 十三香 (page 27) or use store-bought

Salt

Bean curd or tofu

Neutral oil

Gluten Intestine 麵腸 (page 58) or use store-bought, cut crosswise into ½-inch wheels

Soy Chicken 豆雞 (page 61)

King oyster mushrooms

Fresh tofu skin rolls 豆包

Sesame oil 香油, for serving

Chopped cilantro leaves, scallions, and/or fresh red chilies, for garnish

Chili Oil (page 95) or Sweet Chili Sauce (page 17), for dipping

綠豆薏仁 lǜdòu yìrén | lik-tāu-ì-lîn

Mung Bean Soup with Pearl Barley

When pimples break out on my face, my mom prescribes me this sweet soup, which she says can xiāohuǒ (消火), or reduce inflammation. Healthful qualities aside, this is a simple, refreshing summertime treat that you can serve cold by itself or over shaved ice. You can also drink this as a hot soup in the winter, but then I'd swap the mung beans for red adzuki beans and pearl barley for purple rice. Play with the proportions to suit your taste.

Serves 6 to 8

1 cup (200g) dried mung beans 綠豆

½ cup (90g) Chinese pearl barley 薏仁

8⅓ cups water

¼ cup (50g) golden granulated sugar, plus more as needed

1 cup (200g) white rock sugar

1 In two small bowls, soak the mung beans and pearl barley separately for at least 2 hours and up to overnight.

2 Drain the pearl barley and add it to the pot of a rice cooker. Add the water and steam on high for 1 hour. Drain the mung beans and add them to the rice cooker. Steam on high for 40 to 50 minutes more, until the mung beans are tender. Alternatively, if you don't have a rice cooker, you can cook this on the stovetop with the same time and procedure, covered and on a slow boil, stirring occasionally, but especially when cooking the mung beans to make sure nothing sticks to the pot. Add the golden sugar and rock sugar, stirring to dissolve. Taste and adjust the sweetness with golden granulated sugar as desired.

3 Serve hot immediately or refrigerate and serve cold. This keeps in an airtight container in the refrigerator for up to 1 week.

豆花 dòuhuā | tāu-hue

Tofu Pudding with Stewed Peanuts and Sweet Red Beans

Traditional Taiwanese tofu pudding is coagulated with calcium sulfate (gypsum), which yields what I like—curds that have an almost melt-in-your-mouth tenderness. This recipe is served hot, like a soup. You can also serve it cold with some shaved ice. Besides peanuts and red beans, lǜdòu yìrén (Mung Bean Soup with Pearl Barley, page 119) can also be used as a topping, and so can some brown sugar–stewed tapioca pearls.

Note: If you use the dòujiāng (soy milk) recipe on page 74 and still experience sandy tofu pudding, or tofu pudding that just won't coagulate, your cloth is probably not fine enough. Look for nylon cloths; they are often finer than cotton ones. Instead of making your own fresh soy milk, you can also purchase it from an Asian grocery store or an artisanal tofu shop. Ideally, you want soy milk with at least 5g protein per 100ml, and the ingredients should include only soybeans and water.

1 To make the sweet red beans: In a small bowl, soak the red beans with enough water to cover by at least 2 inches for at least 8 hours and up to overnight. Drain the red beans, discarding the water, and add them to the pot of a rice cooker along with the fresh water. Steam for about 1 hour, until the red beans are tender. Transfer the still-hot red beans to a medium mixing bowl. Add the golden and brown sugars and incorporate them into the red beans by pouring the red beans from one bowl to another. The sugar should gradually melt and distribute throughout the red beans without you having to stir, which would rupture the beans. Once the sugar has fully melted, set the beans aside.

2 To make the stewed peanuts: Add the peanuts and water to the pot of a rice cooker and steam for about 4 hours, until they are completely soft and tender. You can also cook them on the stovetop, but make sure the

(continued)

Serves 6 to 8

Sweet Red Beans 蜜紅豆

1¼ cups (250g) dried red adzuki beans

2 cups water

½ cup (100g) golden granulated sugar

2 Tbsp (25g) dark brown sugar 黑糖

Stewed Peanuts

1¼ cups (250g) unsalted raw, shelled peanuts

2 cups water

¼ cup (50g) golden granulated sugar

Sweet Syrup 糖水

2½ cups water

¼ cup (50g) white rock sugar

½ cup (100g) golden granulated sugar

1 (1½-inch) piece unpeeled ginger (20g), cut into ¼-inch slices (optional)

(continued)

Tofu Pudding with Stewed Peanuts and
Sweet Red Beans ——— continued

water doesn't boil too rapidly. Transfer the contents in the rice cooker to a small pot set over medium heat. Add the golden granulated sugar and boil for 5 to 10 minutes, to emulsify the soup (it should turn from clear to white) and infuse the sweetness. Don't stir too much, as the peanuts can easily break apart. Set aside.

3 To make the sweet syrup: In a saucepan set over high heat, combine the water, rock sugar, golden sugar, and ginger (if using). Bring to a boil, then lower the heat to medium-low and simmer for 5 to 10 minutes, until you can smell the fragrance of the sugar (and the kick of ginger, if using). Set aside.

4 To make the tofu pudding: In a medium lidded pot, combine the calcium sulfate, sweet potato starch, and cold water to make the coagulant. Stir well to make sure everything is dissolved and set aside. In a separate pot over medium-high heat, warm the unsweetened soy milk until it reaches 185°F (85°C), stirring constantly to ensure it doesn't burn on the bottom. Once the soy milk is hot, stir the coagulant once more and pour the soy milk all at once and from a high point into the pot with the coagulant so everything is distributed evenly throughout. Cover with the lid, remove from the heat, and let sit for 20 minutes, until completely set.

5 Scoop the tofu pudding with a flat soup ladle at a roughly 20-degree angle and invert it into a shallow serving bowl. Ladle the warm syrup over it and top with stewed peanuts and sweet red beans. Serve immediately.

Tofu Pudding

2 tsp (5g) calcium sulfate 硫酸鈣

2 Tbsp (16g) fine sweet potato starch 細地瓜粉

10 tsp (50g) cold water

4 cups unsweetened Soy Milk 豆漿 (page 74) or use store-bought

Vegetables

There's a dracaena plant in my dad's Maryland home; it has been there since he emigrated as a fifteen-year-old. It had wide, curvy emerald-green leaves that resembled kelp. A-Gong didn't always approve of my mom marrying into the family. But my mom was determined to prove her worth. She watered the dracaena for the nine years that she dated my dad. The year they married, it bloomed with clusters of dandelion-like white flowers and perfumed the entire home with a sweet fragrance. Nobody knew it was even possible for the plant to flower.

My mom emigrated with her parents to Maryland when she was fourteen years old. She returned almost twenty years later, to live with A-Gong and the rest of my paternal family, having never stepped foot in a Taiwanese market and having ten new mouths to feed.

She spent the following years frequenting the traditional markets and acquiring not only bargaining skills but also the eye required for singling out the best produce. (Don't worry, Mom, I kept the numbers vague to keep your age a secret.) She made friends with all the vendors, so every time I went with her, it felt like we were famous people. Everyone remembered the little kid who hung out with the crowd of aunties and grandmas at the break of dawn.

"It isn't gracious to a vendor if you keep fondling the produce," my mom would say. "Each time you touch it with your hands, the quality deteriorates." Instead, she taught me to use my eyes and senses. She taught me that daikon radishes with thin, straight cracks on the body and crisp green tops were the sweetest, and they made the most incredible *tshài-thâu-kué* (Turnip Cake, page 234) with just rice and salt. She picked the youngest dark purple eggplants that peeked white under the stem leaves and had no green scars. When she prepared and cooked them, they had minimal seeds, and their pearly, tender flesh tasted refreshingly sweet. She gave me a variety of other tips: green vegetables can't have any trace of yellowing; bamboo shoots can't have green on the tip sheaths or they'll be bitter; bitter melons will be bitter, but those with larger bumps are less so; mushrooms need to look and feel firm; and bean sprouts need their roots removed to stay fresh longer.

We didn't live or eat extravagantly, but the dining table was always filled with the day's produce. Dishes were never overly tasty. I just remember everything made me feel good. The simplest stir-fried greens gleamed and the flavors sung. An emulsion of oil and the vegetable's juices clung to each blade or leaf. Sometimes half the garlic was too charred, half was barely cooked. I liked it imperfect that way. Those plates were always the first to empty.

Stir-Frying Vegetables

It isn't a surprise that the finest Taiwanese restaurants feature their vegetables using the same simple techniques a home cook uses. The key to delicious stir-fried vegetables is using just a few seasonings and quick technique to retain their vitality, nutrients, and original tastes. In our home, we generally don't use anything other than aromatics (typically sliced or minced garlic and ginger), salt, and pepper. At most, we'll add a very small drizzle of rice cooking wine or black vinegar near the end of stir-frying. For grassier or inherently bitter vegetables like a-cài (Taiwanese lettuce) and bōcài (Taiwanese spinach), we'll use a larger proportion of aromatics and occasionally throw in a few red chilies (minced or sliced on the bias) at the start to kiss all the vegetables with spice, or last for garnish. There are certain ingredient combinations we rarely change. Green cabbage is served with slivers of carrot, amaranth greens with fresh tofu skin, dòumiáo (pea shoots) with a splash of Shaoxing wine, and mung bean sprouts with sliced garlic and hefty cracks of black pepper. Here are some general tips for stir-frying vegetables:

1 Wash all your vegetables and drain them well. Pick, trim, and separate the tender leaves from the thicker stems. Get your mise en place ready, and keep your neutral oil, aromatics, and seasonings close to the stove. Consider blanching vegetables like gai lan, green beans, and eggplants (see page 144) that have tougher skins and tissues in water or oil.

2 Set your wok over the highest heat. Ladle in neutral oil and swirl it around to create a nonstick surface. Add the aromatics and cook for 2 to 5 seconds, just until fragrant. Add the thicker stems and stir constantly to coat the pieces with oil for 15 to 30 seconds, until they begin to release moisture and look alive. Add the rest of the greens, taking care not to overcrowd the wok. Mix and toss the greens and season them with salt or other seasonings. Continue stir-frying and tossing rapidly until the greens are just wilted, 1 to 2 minutes. Add a small splash of water if things are looking too dry. Add in the other accompaniments, such as slivers of carrots. Toss a few more times to finish.

3 Transfer to a plate and serve immediately.

涼筍 liángsǔn

Bamboo Salad

To me, this is a dish that tastes like summer. Green bamboo shoot (in Taiwanese, *lík-tik-sún*) season starts at the beginning of May. The shoots are so crisp, juicy, and sweet that you may wonder why pears even exist. Bamboo shoots and mayo seem like an odd pairing, but this is precisely how A-Gong liked it. Instead of mayo, some also prefer Garlic Soy Paste (page 101) as an accompaniment, the classic before mayo was popularized.

1 For fresh bamboo shoots, do this first step as soon as you return home from the market. The shoots can grow bitter if you let them sit around uncooked. Rinse any dirt off the shoots. In a large pot, combine the bamboos shoots and 8⅓ cups water, or enough to cover the bamboo shoots. Cover the pot and bring to a boil. (You can add a spoonful of raw rice or a splash of rice-washing water [洗米水; see page 35] plus a whole mild red chili to the water. This addition helps suppress the natural bitterness that some may find unpalatable.) Lower the heat to maintain a gentle boil, cover, and continue to cook for 35 to 40 minutes, or until you can smell the fragrance of the bamboo. Drain and let cool. Refrigerate in airtight bags until ready to use, up to 3 days.

2 To make the mayonnaise dressing: In a tall cup or bowl, combine the soy milk, neutral oil, lemon juice, sugar, and salt. Using an immersion blender, blend for about 10 seconds, until thick and emulsified. Taste and adjust the seasoning as needed; alter the balance of lemon juice and sugar as you please. Add to a piping bag and set aside.

3 Pry the bamboo shoot open with your fingers and remove the shell (save the tip for garnish). Trim and discard the bottom, then use a vegetable peeler to peel off the bumpy exterior of the shoot. Roll-cut each shoot into 1-inch chunks and place on a serving plate. Pipe the mayonnaise in a zigzag pattern onto the bamboo chunks. Garnish with the tip of the shoot and serve.

Serves 6 as part of a spread

3 fresh bamboo shoots, preferably green bamboo shoots, 綠竹筍 (1,200g, about 700g after shelling and trimming), or use precooked and vacuum-packed

Mayonnaise Dressing
沙拉醬

2 Tbsp unsweetened Soy Milk 豆漿 (page 74) or use store-bought plus soy lecithin powder, as needed, for emulsifying

¼ cup neutral oil

2 tsp lemon juice, plus more as needed

1½ Tbsp (23g) granulated golden sugar, plus more as needed

¼ tsp salt

黄金泡菜 *huángjīn pàocài*

Golden Kimchi

When I make this kimchi, I think about how the world's cuisines are more alike than we tend to believe. Instead of the gochugaru (Korean chili flakes) and fish sauce or shrimp paste that are used in Korean kimchi, this Taiwanese-style kimchi makes use of local flavors with spicy fermented bean curd. It is just as savory, garlicky, and pungent but takes only one day to ferment. Kabocha squash isn't necessarily a common addition, but I find that it brings a source of natural sweetness and freshness to the kimchi.

1 Cut the head of the napa cabbage into 2-inch cubes. (Save the root for shàngtāng, Superior Stock, on page 151; you can freeze the root until you're ready to use it.) Inspect the leaves, especially the ones situated near the center of the head, and remove any with gray or brown discolored spots. Rinse the cabbage pieces and drain them well. Place the napa cabbage, thinly sliced carrots, and daikon radish in a large bowl and sprinkle them with the salt. Rub the salt in well and let sit at room temperature for at least 2 hours. If possible, give them a stir every 30 to 45 minutes to evenly distribute the salt.

2 To make the pickling paste: In a wok or pan set over medium heat, warm the sesame oil. Add the kabocha squash and let it sweat for 2 to 3 minutes. Add the carrot cubes and cook until both the squash and carrots are just tender but still hold a little resistance when pierced with a paring knife. You don't want the carrots and squash to brown, so keep an eye and turn down the heat if anything starts to caramelize. Stir in the sugar. Mix and toss so that all the sugar melts, coats each piece of vegetable, and gives off just a light caramel scent. Transfer to a bowl and set aside to cool. In a blender, combine the cooled carrots and squash, garlic, ginger, red chili, spicy fermented bean curd, and rice vinegar and blend until smooth. Set aside.

Makes one 7½-cup jar

1 large head napa cabbage (1,200g)

½ carrot (100g), thinly sliced with a peeler

¼ peeled daikon radish (100g), thinly sliced with a peeler

3 Tbsp (50g) salt, preferably a coarse non-iodized pickling salt

2 fresh red chilies (20g), sliced on a bias

Pickling Paste

2 Tbsp sesame oil 香油 (or use oil from the fermented bean curd)

½ kabocha squash (200g), cut into ½-inch cubes

1 carrot (200g), cut into ½-inch cubes

⅓ cup (65g) golden granulated sugar

10 garlic cloves (30g)

1 (1-inch) piece peeled ginger, roughly chopped

3 Discard the water that has gathered beneath the cabbage, carrots, and daikon radish. They should now feel limp and look slightly translucent. Rinse the vegetables once to get rid of excess salt. Drain and dry them very well.

4 In a large bowl, combine the napa cabbage, carrots, daikon radish, sliced red chilies, and pickling paste. Using clean hands, massage the paste in, making sure it coats every piece of vegetable. Pack the kimchi into a lidded 7½-cup glass container. Press down while packing to push out all the air bubbles.

5 Let ferment in the refrigerator for at least 1 day before serving, and store in the fridge for up to 1 month. It is best served cold!

1 fresh red chili (10g), roughly chopped

2 small cubes spicy fermented bean curd in sesame oil 麻油辣腐乳 (24g)

½ cup rice vinegar

梅漬小番茄 méizì xiǎofānqié

Plum Pickled Cherry Tomatoes

In Taiwan's grueling summers, it's hard to build up an appetite. These pickled cherry tomatoes are the perfect side dish for these sweltering times, bursting with the lovely sourness of suānméi (Taiwanese dried plums). Look for fresh and plump cherry tomatoes, which should have skins that peel off easily after they're blanched. Taste the pickling liquid and adjust the flavor as necessary: you want a balance between the salty, sweet, and sour notes, and also a strong taste so that the tomatoes will soak up enough flavor. The pickling liquid can also be diluted with ice water to make a refreshing drink!

Makes one 2-cup jar

2¼ cups water

15 Taiwanese dried plums 話梅/酸梅 (60g)

¼ cup (50g) white rock sugar, plus more as needed

¼ cup lemon juice, plus more as needed

21 oz (600g) cherry tomatoes, stems removed

1 In a saucepan, combine the water, dried plums, and rock sugar. Bring to a low simmer over medium heat, and cook for 4 to 5 minutes, until the water turns a golden color and the flavor of the plums permeates throughout. Set aside to cool. Stir the lemon juice into the cooled mixture. Taste and adjust the sweetness and tartness as desired.

2 Prepare a bowl of ice water to shock the cherry tomatoes. Bring a medium pot of water to a boil over high heat. Add the tomatoes and blanch for 30 seconds. Using a slotted spoon or spider strainer, quickly transfer them to the ice water to stop the cooking.

3 Most of the tomatoes' skins should peel back in the ice water, but for the tomatoes that still have skins intact, peel them with a paring knife from the stem end. Be careful not to pierce through the flesh of the tomatoes. Rinse off bits of residue in the ice water bath. Place the tomatoes in a lidded 2-cup jar and add the pickling liquid and all the plums. Secure the lid and refrigerate for at least 2 days before enjoying. Store for up to 1 week. Serve cold as a side.

燙地瓜葉 tàng dìguāyè

Blanched Sweet Potato Leaves

Besides qīngchǎo (plain stir-frying) or suànchǎo (frying with garlic), tàng (blanching) is another common way in which vegetables are prepared in Taiwan. "Blanching" refers to a quick dip in boiling water to just wilt the vegetable and retain its freshness and nutrients. This, in Taiwan, is usually followed with tossing the vegetables with soy sauce flavored with fried shallots. If you don't have pickled garlic on hand, you can fry fresh garlic (or ginger if you are allium-free, as are Taiwanese Buddhist vegetarians) in a little oil and add a pinch of sugar. The braising liquid and bits from sùlǔfàn (Braised Pork, page 173) make a great topping as well. You can also use this method with a-cài (Taiwanese lettuce), bōcài (Taiwanese spinach), and kōngxīncài (water spinach).

Serves 4 as part of a spread

10½ oz (300g) sweet potato leaves 地瓜葉

5 Pickled Garlic cloves 糖蒜 (page 18), plus 1 tsp of the brine

2 tsp light soy sauce

1 tsp (5g) Fried Shallots 油蔥 (page 175)

½ tsp salt

1 tsp neutral oil

1 Wash the sweet potato leaves, wring them dry, and snap off the lower portion of each stalk that feels tougher than the rest. The pieces you want to keep should snap off cleanly. Pick off any portions that are extra fibrous.

2 In a medium bowl, combine the pickled garlic and its brine, the light soy sauce, and fried shallots. Set the sauce aside.

3 In a pot, bring 4 cups water to a rolling boil. Add the salt and neutral oil to the water (the oil helps prevent the leaves from blackening). Add the sweet potato leaves and blanch them for 5 to 10 seconds, until the leaves turn a vibrant green and are just wilted. (If you use a vegetable other than sweet potato leaves, such as water spinach, with thicker stems that take longer to cook, drop the stem portions in the water first to give them a head start.)

4 Using a spider strainer or a large slotted spoon, transfer the sweet potato leaves to the bowl with the sauce. Don't worry about draining the leaves here; carrying some water (about 1 Tbsp) helps keep the leaves moist and distributes the sauce. Toss quickly to coat the sweet potato leaves with the sauce. Transfer to a plate and serve.

腐乳空心菜 fǔrǔ kōngxīncài

Water Spinach with Fermented Bean Curd

This dish is testament that everyone needs a jar of tiánjiǔ dòufǔrǔ (Sweet Wine Fermented Bean Curd, page 52) in their pantry. It brings a decadent savory flavor to even the simplest of stir-fried vegetables, and combining it with water spinach feels like a match made in heaven. Change up the flavor with your fermented bean curd. If your fermented bean curd doesn't taste much of mǐjiǔ (rice cooking wine), I recommend adding a small splash of it during the stir-fry.

1 Wash the water spinach, wring it dry, and trim off the lower portion of the stalk that feels tougher than the rest (generally, a 2- to 4-inch portion). Cut the water spinach into 2- to 2½-inch-long segments.

2 In a small dish, mash the fermented bean curd and its sauce (get a few grains of the rice and/or soybeans in there as well) into a smooth mixture. Set aside.

3 Set a wok over high heat and heat it until it just starts smoking. Ladle in the neutral oil and swirl it around to create a nonstick surface. Add the garlic and red chili and cook for 2 to 5 seconds, just until fragrant. Add the water spinach and quickly follow with the fermented bean curd sauce. Stir-fry and toss rapidly for 1 to 2 minutes, until the water spinach is just wilted. Transfer to a plate and serve immediately.

Serves 4 to 6 as part of a spread

21 oz (600g) water spinach 空心菜, about 500g after trimming

1 large cube Sweet Wine Fermented Bean Curd 豆腐乳 (page 52) or use store-bought (16g), plus 2 tsp of the sauce

1 Tbsp neutral oil

3 garlic cloves, minced

1 fresh red chili, sliced on a bias

番茄花椰菜 fānqié huāyécài

Tomato and Cauliflower Stir-Fry

The Taiwanese variety of "flowering" cauliflower is similar to Fioretto cauliflower, with small flower buds that sit atop long stems. They are sweeter and more tender than your average cauliflower and perfect for stir-frying. When stir-fried with tomatoes, garlic, and scallions, it has a light, gentle umami taste. If you want it more strongly flavored, try stewing the tomatoes longer or adding a small spoonful of ketchup. In place of scallions, Buddhist vegetarians can use snap peas; add them at the final moments of cooking to retain their crunch.

Serves 4 to 6 as part of a spread

2 medium tomatoes (300g)

1 head (550g) cauliflower, preferably Taiwanese or "flowering" cauliflower, trimmed into bite-size florets

2 Tbsp neutral oil

3 garlic cloves or 1 (1-inch) piece peeled ginger, minced

2 scallions (30g), cut into 2-inch segments, white and green parts separated

½ cup water

1 tsp golden granulated sugar

1 tsp salt

Pinch of white pepper

1 Core the tomatoes and make a 1-inch X in the opposite bottom end with a small paring knife.

2 Bring a pot of water to a boil. Blanch the cauliflower for 1 minute and, using a spider strainer or slotted spoon, transfer it to a plate. Blanch the tomatoes for 30 to 45 seconds, until their skins begin to visibly peel back. Remove the tomatoes with a spider or slotted spoon and rinse them under cold water until cool. Peel off the skin and cut each tomato into six to eight wedges.

3 Set a wok over medium-high heat and heat it until it just starts smoking. Ladle in the neutral oil and swirl it around to create a nonstick surface. Add the garlic and scallion whites and cook for 10 seconds, until fragrant. Add the tomatoes and toss a few times. Add the water, bring to a boil (if it doesn't boil immediately), and then lower the heat to medium. Cover and cook for about 1 minute, until the tomatoes have softened. Add the cauliflower, sugar, and salt. Toss a few times, then cover and cook for 3 to 4 minutes more, until the cauliflower is at your desired crunchiness. Add the scallion greens and give everything a few more tosses. Sprinkle with a pinch of white pepper, transfer the vegetables and their liquids to a plate, and serve. Cool any leftovers and store in the refrigerator for up to 3 days.

雪菜豆乾 xuěcài dòugān

Preserved Greens and Bean Curd Stir-Fry

This dish makes me nostalgic about the bento boxes I had in elementary school. In Taiwan's humidity, a plain stir-fried cabbage can spoil and turn sour, so xuěcài often fills the vegetable compartment in our bento boxes. Its salty fragrance permeates throughout the bean curd and edamame, so you won't need additional salt. In place of xuěcài, try also suāncài (Fermented Mustard Greens, page 35) to bring acidity and a different fragrance.

1 Bring a pot of water to a gentle boil over medium-high heat. Add the edamame and cook for about 3 minutes, until the bean taste is less prevalent and it is still crunchy (taste one to check). Drain the beans and rinse them with water until cool to the touch. Rub the edamame between your fingers to release and remove their skins. Set aside.

2 Gently rinse the preserved greens to mellow any excess salt without ridding the greens of their prized flavor. Chop into a ¼-inch mince. The leaves can get tangled; chop them a few more times so they won't be in long strands.

3 Heat a wok over medium-high heat until just smoking. Ladle in the neutral oil and swirl it around to create a nonstick surface. Add the bean curd and stir-fry for 1 to 2 minutes, until the edges are lightly golden. Add the ginger and red chili and stir-fry for 15 to 30 seconds to release their fragrances. Swirl in the soy sauce and add the sugar. Fry the bean curd in the soy sauce for about 1 minute, until the soy sauce's fragrance has deepened. Add the minced preserved greens and stir-fry everything together for 1 minute, until you can smell the greens. Add the edamame and stir-fry for another minute, or until most of the steam dissipates and the greens appear crunchy. To finish, drizzle in the sesame oil, sprinkle on a pinch of white pepper, transfer to a serving dish, and serve immediately.

Serves 4 to 6 as part of a spread

½ cup (100g) shelled edamame (green soybeans) 毛豆

7 oz (200g) Preserved Greens 雪菜 (page 41) or use store-bought

1 Tbsp neutral oil

2 blocks dark bean curd 黑豆乾 (150g), cut into ½-inch cubes

2 tsp peeled and minced ginger

1 fresh small red chili (5g), cut into thin rings

1 tsp light soy sauce

½ tsp golden granulated sugar

1 tsp sesame oil 香油

Pinch of white pepper

薑絲菜瓜 jiāngsī càiguā | kiunn-si tshài-kue

Loofah Stir-Fried with Ginger

There is no vegetable that reminds me of home better than loofah. They are cheap and easy to grow; the loofah we ate at home usually came from A-Gong's garden. He cooked it with *tāu-tshiam* (豆簽), a type of noodle made with powdered black-eyed peas, and added no condiments other than salt. Savory juices are released from the loofah into the noodle cooking water, and you end up with a naturally thickened soup. When you're preparing the ingredients for this dish, cut the loofah last to preserve its freshness. Try to find young ginger, the kind with pale yellow skin and pink tips that won't overpower the subtle flavors of the loofah. To make this a main dish, you can mix in some salty miànxiàn (Taiwanese long-life noodles) in place of salt and add a source of protein such as tofu.

1 Trim off both ends of the loofah and peel the skin with a vegetable peeler. Quarter it lengthwise and cut into ½-inch chunks.

2 Set a saucepan over the stove and fill it with the water. Bring to a boil and remove from the heat. Cover with a lid to keep the water warm.

3 Set a wok over medium heat and heat it until it just starts smoking. Ladle in the neutral oil and swirl the oil around to create a nonstick surface. Add the garlic (if using), ginger, and yellow onion and stir-fry them to release their fragrances, about 15 seconds. Add the loofah and gently and quickly stir to evenly distribute all the aromatics. Swirl the rice cooking wine around the sides of the wok and follow with the reserved hot water. Cover the wok and let cook for 2 to 3 minutes, until all the loofah pieces are tender and their once white flesh turns shiny and translucent. Season with salt and quickly stir and swirl very gently to evenly distribute the salt, being careful not to smush the now-tender loofah. The loofah discolors quickly, so work fast! Transfer to a plate and serve immediately.

Serves 4 to 6 as part of a spread

1 loofah 菜瓜/絲瓜 (650g)

½ cup water

1 Tbsp neutral oil

3 garlic cloves, minced (optional)

1 (1½-inch) piece young ginger 嫩薑 (15g), or half the amount of older ginger, julienned

¼ yellow onion (50g), thinly sliced

2 Tbsp Taiwanese rice cooking wine

½ tsp salt

塔香茄子 tǎxiāng qiézi

Basil-Fragrant Eggplants

This dish is an adaptation of the famed Sichuanese dish yúxiāng ("fish-fragrant") eggplants. It accents the aroma of Taiwanese basil while keeping the umami, spice, tang, and sweet notes of the original version. Instead of textured vegetable protein, you can also use crumbled firm tofu.

Serves 4 to 6 as part of a spread

2 Asian long eggplants (400g total)

1¾ cups plus 1 Tbsp water

2 Tbsp rice vinegar

¼ tsp salt

1½ Tbsp (10g) textured vegetable protein mince (TVP) 素肉丁

About 1 cup neutral oil, for frying

½ tsp potato starch or cornstarch

8 garlic cloves, minced, or 1 Tbsp peeled and minced ginger

1 tsp Fermented Chili Paste 辣椒醬 (page 16)

1 Tbsp dòubànjiàng (chili bean paste) 豆瓣醬

½ Tbsp light soy sauce

2 tsp granulated sugar

1 handful (about 15g) Taiwanese basil leaves 九層塔 or Thai basil leaves

1 Trim both ends off each eggplant. Cut them crosswise into 2½-inch segments and halve those segments twice lengthwise to create batons. In a large bowl, combine the eggplant, 1 cup of the water, the rice vinegar, and salt. Stir to coat all the pieces and let soak for 10 minutes. Drain the eggplant batons and set them aside.

2 In a small bowl filled with hot water, soak the TVP for about 10 minutes, until springy and expanded. Drain into a sieve. Rinse and squeeze the TVP until its liquid runs clear. Set aside.

3 Line a plate with paper towels. In a wok over medium-high heat, warm the neutral oil to 355°F (180°C). Fry the eggplants in three or four separate batches to avoid overcrowding. Fry each batch for 1 to 2 minutes, until the skins are deeply purple and the white flesh just starts to caramelize at the edges. Using a spider strainer or slotted spoon, transfer each batch to the towel-lined plates to drain.

4 In a small bowl, make a slurry with the potato starch and 1 Tbsp of the water. Mix until no lumps remain and set aside.

5 Pour out all but 1 to 2 Tbsp of the oil in the wok and heat over medium heat. Add the TVP and fry for 3 to 5 minutes, until just golden. Add the garlic, fermented chili paste, and dòubànjiàng and fry to stain the oil red, 1 to 2 minutes. Swirl in the light soy sauce. Add the remaining ¾ cup water and the sugar and bring to a boil. Add the fried eggplants back in and toss a few times. Stir the slurry to make sure it's incorporated and drizzle it into the mixture to thicken the sauce. Remove the wok from the heat and add the basil. Taste and adjust the seasoning as needed. Transfer to a plate and serve immediately.

Soups

At A-Gong's table, we always had soup. No spread is complete without something hot and brothy—it's just as important as the rice. We have soup year-round, in all types of weather. Sipping hot broth in the skin-crawling summer heat with beads of sweat obscuring your vision is all part of the romance. The spread is built around the soup. When there are heavier or fried dishes, we pair them with clear, refreshing soups. When there is a hearty main, we have simpler and lighter soups.

Stocks

Stocks are the foundation of this book. They build the framework not just for soups but for many dishes. Vegetarian meat doesn't supply flavor like meat does, so you may often find yourself wanting a little more of something—a stock can achieve this. A good stock contributes not just umami flavor but also body and complexity. It shouldn't be so flavorful that it overpowers everything and makes all your dishes taste the same, and it shouldn't be too salty so your dishes stay flexible with seasoning. You also don't want it to be so dark-colored that it makes food look unappetizing.

Taiwanese cuisine has its roots in Fujian and draws many elements of flavor construction from Japan. That is why, funnily, Chinese tourists (especially Northerners) often find Taiwanese food to be a blander version of Chinese food—less oil, less salt, more original flavors. That said, it's common for Taiwanese recipes to use elements of Japanese soup stocks: nonvegetarian *mī-suànn-kôo* (Mee Sua, page 168) famously deploys katsuobushi (bonito flakes), a remnant of colonial times. I find that kombu—a key ingredient in Japanese dashi—is the most agreeable vegetarian base for Taiwanese cooking. It supplies that briny and elegant umami flavor that seafood typically has. The dried shiitake mushroom, another Japanese dashi ingredient, is also great but can be slightly less versatile as it sometimes overpowers dishes. Soybean sprouts, on the other hand, are great for making a balanced stock. Unlike dried soybeans, they make a soup that is clear and a very attractive golden color.

I don't like to use too many ingredients that are perfectly good for eating in my stocks. So for something like gāotāng (All-Purpose Stock, page 150), rather than using typical stock ingredients like daikon radish, carrots, and ears of corn, I'll make use of the stems of fresh shiitake mushrooms, the outer leaves of green cabbage, and the core and peel of pineapples—parts that we often trim off and throw out. Think about taking from fruits and vegetables that can lend umami and sweetness to broth. There is lots of room for you to make this stock yours.

高湯 gāotāng | 母湯 bú-thng

All-Purpose Stock

This is a light, golden stock with a gentle umami flavor that works well for all kinds of dishes. If you can't find soybean sprouts (do not substitute mung bean sprouts) at your local Asian grocery, increase the amount of kombu to 10g per liter. If you foresee using this stock a lot, double the concentration (double all the ingredients while keeping the water level the same). You can dilute the stock with some water before using, or keep it as is and enjoy a supercharged stock!

1 Rinse the soybean sprouts and the mushroom stems (if using). Pick out any bad or discolored soybeans and remove any black spots or debris from the mushrooms.

2 In a tall pot, bring the water to a rolling boil over high heat. Add the soybean sprouts and mushroom stems. Lower the heat so it is just barely bubbling, cover, and boil for 2 hours, until the broth has taken on a golden hue and reduced to about 10 cups.

3 Remove the pot from the heat. While the broth is still hot but not boiling, add the kombu. Cover and let the kombu soak for 2 hours. This is just enough time to extract its umami flavors without letting the seaweed odor become overpowering.

4 Remove the kombu using a slotted spoon or spider strainer. Using a cheesecloth–lined sieve, strain the stock into another large pot. Once it's cool enough to touch, twist and squeeze the tofu cloth (with the soybean sprouts and mushroom stems in it), extracting as much of the stock and flavor as possible. Season the stock with the salt. The stock is very lightly salted and will taste flat, but its flavors will come alive once you add it to a seasoned dish. Cool completely, then store in the refrigerator for up to 3 days or freeze the stock in a few separate resealable bags for ease of access for up to 3 months. You may want to strain the stock again after defrosting, as some kombu debris can come out of the solution.

Makes about 10 cups

14 oz (400g) soybean sprouts 黄豆芽 (not mung bean sprouts)

10 fresh shiitake mushroom stems (about 40g; optional)

12½ cups water

6 (5-inch) pieces kombu (20g)

¼ tsp salt

上湯 shàngtāng

Superior Stock

Some Taiwanese soups get their signature flavor from searing meat and dissolving the caramelized bits at the bottom of the pot into the broth. This brown stock is made from a medley of roasted vegetables, which mimics that process. It is balanced, rich, full-bodied, and a great base for more heavily flavored broths, particularly ones where beef or duck are originally in place.

1 Preheat the oven to 390°F (200°C), with convection on if available.

2 On one or two baking trays, spread the fresh mushrooms, cherry tomatoes, napa cabbage core, ginger, carrot, and scallions in a single layer. Roast for 22 to 25 minutes, until all the pieces are deep golden brown.

3 Fill a tall pot with the water and add the roasted vegetables. While the baking tray is still hot, add about 2 Tbsp water, gently scrape up any brown bits, and add this caramel-brown water to the pot. Add the dried shiitakes, daikon radish, yellow onions, celery, and minced preserved cabbage. In a small bowl, using a bit of the stock from the pot, mash up the fermented bean curd to a slurry. Add the slurry to the pot. Turn the heat to high and bring the broth to a rolling boil. Lower the heat slightly so it is still bubbling but not as rapidly. Cover and cook for 3 hours, until the stock reduces to about 10 cups.

4 Strain the stock through a tofu-cloth-lined sieve into another pot. Once it's cooled, twist and squeeze the vegetables in the cloth and extract as much of the stock and flavor as possible. The stock won't taste salty enough, but this is intentional; you'll lose seasoning flexibility in later dishes if you salt it now. Cool completely and store in the refrigerator for up to 3 days, or freeze the stock in a few separate resealable bags for ease of access for up to 3 months.

Makes about 10 cups

7 oz (200g) fresh mushrooms such as shiitake, shimeji, and oyster

⅔ cup (100g) cherry tomatoes

Core portion of 1 large napa cabbage (350g), quartered

1 (3-inch) piece peeled ginger (50g), cut into ¼-inch-thick slices

1 unpeeled carrot (200g), cut into 1-inch chunks

2 scallions (30g), both white and green parts, cut into 2-inch segments

12½ cups water

14 dried shiitake mushrooms (35g)

½ peeled daikon radish (300g), cut into 1-inch chunks

1 yellow onion (200g), halved

1 stalk celery (40g)

2 Tbsp (25g) non-spicy preserved cabbage 冬菜, minced

2 cubes (32g) Sweet Wine Fermented Bean Curd 豆腐乳 (page 52) or use store-bought

竹筍湯 zhúsǔntāng │ tik-sún-thng

Bamboo Soup

Bamboo soup was a staple on A-Gong's table. He made it with just three ingredients: pork ribs, bamboo shoots, and water. That simple, humble quality is something I try to honor, even when making a vegetarian version. Preserved winter melon supplies a sweet, complex fragrance that goes well with the bamboo, and it's all you need. Instead of the preserved winter melon, you can also use a few slabs of preserved oriental melon sliced into batons. Cook what's in season: in Taiwan, this means green bamboo shoots (綠竹筍) in the summer and winter bamboo shoots (冬筍) in the winter.

Serves 6 as part of a spread

2.2 lb (1,000g) fresh bamboo shoots (about 500g after shelling and trimming)

6¼ cups water

1 piece (30g) Winter Melon in Soybean Sauce 醬冬瓜 (page 45) or use store-bought

1½ tsp salt

1 Pry each bamboo shoot open with your fingers and remove the shell. Trim off the bottom and use a vegetable peeler to peel off the bumpy exterior of each shoot. At a small slant along the base, roll-cut the shoots into ½-inch-thick slices (at the thickest part).

2 Fill a medium pot with the water. Add the sliced bamboo, cover the pot, and bring to a boil over high heat. Lower the heat to low or medium-low to maintain a slow boil, cover, and cook for 30 minutes.

3 Add the winter melon to a braising pouch or a small piece of cheesecloth (do this if the preserved winter melon is too soft, as it can disintegrate and cloud up the soup) and tie a knot to secure it. Add the winter melon and salt to the pot and cook, covered, for 30 minutes more. At the end, taste and adjust the soup's seasoning as needed before serving in bowls. Discard the braising pouch (if one was used). Cool any leftovers and store in the refrigerator for up to 3 days.

蓮藕湯 liánǒutāng | liân-ngāu-thng

Lotus Root Soup

My mom, who grew up in Kaohsiung, often tells me over this bowl of soup how much she loved water caltrops as a kid. Back in the day, you could find the bat-shaped nuts sold on pushcarts all over the city. Vendors steamed the nuts, then cracked open the shells to reveal the fluffy, starchy kernel. Water caltrops have the texture of potatoes but a distinct musky aroma and a savory, mildly sweet flavor that is reminiscent of peanuts and chestnuts. Few kids could resist their allure. My mom would spend hours prying the shells open, trying to suck out every last bit stuck in the "horns" of the shell. After marrying my dad and moving to Taipei, she tells me it was a lot harder to find those pushcarts, let alone the gothic-looking pods. They've become a thing of the past, but she hasn't forgotten their allure. Whenever she makes lotus root soup, she throws in a few water caltrops right at the end, and it's the only combination I've ever known. The two are all you need to make a wonderfully savory and fragrant clear soup. Its simplicity makes for an almost thoughtless memory reserved for the children in our hearts.

Serves 6 as part of a spread

2 segments lotus root (about 500g and 370g after trimming and peeling)

6¼ cups water

1 Tbsp rice vinegar 糯米醋

12 shelled and cooked water caltrops 菱角 (120g)

1 tsp salt, plus more as needed

1 Trim and peel the lotus root, then cut it into ¼-inch-thick slices. In a large bowl, quickly rinse the sliced lotus roots in 2 cups water and the rice vinegar. Drain and set aside.

2 Fill a tall pot with the water and bring it to a boil over high heat. Add the lotus roots, cover, and lower the heat to a slow boil for 1 to 1½ hours, until they are tender with a slight but not crunchy bite. If you have a pressure cooker, cook over medium heat for 30 minutes.

3 Add the water caltrops and salt to the pot and cook for 5 minutes to infuse all the flavors. Adjust the salt to taste, transfer the soup to a bowl, and serve. Cool any leftovers and store in the refrigerator for up to 3 days.

冬瓜丸子湯 dōngguā wánzitāng

Winter Melon Soup with Tofu Balls

Winter melon paired with ginger is a classic, refreshing combination, and tofu balls are a fun addition to this beloved classic. These tofu balls are reminiscent of the gòngwán (Taiwanese meatballs) I used to eat and love growing up. As long as your tofu doesn't have too much moisture to begin with, it can be mashed and formed into balls without starch and still have a bouncy, tender bite. Opt for plain white dòugān (白豆乾), which is pressed and firmer than any regular tofu. You can add the tofu balls to any soup or hot pot, or you can use them in place of fried tofu in braised dishes such as lǔwèi (Soy-Braised Goods, page 116). You can also serve them crispy with a dipping sauce, such as soy sauce paste (pages 111–112) and haishan sauce (page 108). See photograph for the tofu balls on page 204.

1 To make the tofu balls: In a small bowl, soak the dried shiitake mushrooms in warm water to cover until fully soft, 20 to 30 minutes. Drain and discard the water, snip off the stems, and mince the caps.

2 In the bowl of a food processor, process the bean curd for 1 to 2 minutes to a fine paste. The paste should almost have a bounce when you tap on the side of the bowl of the food processor. If you don't have a food processor, you can achieve a similar effect by pressing and grinding the bean curd with the flat side of a cleaver. Transfer the bean curd paste to a large bowl and add the minced mushrooms, minced ginger, jicama, salt, sugar, white pepper, and mushroom powder (if using). Mix to combine thoroughly and divide it evenly into twelve portions (about 30g each). Using wet hands, roll each portion into a smooth ball.

3 Line a plate with paper towels. In a wok over medium-high heat, warm the neutral oil to 355°F (180°C). Add the tofu balls and fry until golden brown, 2 to 3 minutes. Using a slotted spoon, transfer the tofu balls to the towel-lined plate.

Serves 6 as part of a spread

Tofu Balls (makes 12)

6 dried shiitake mushrooms (15g)

10½ oz (300g) white bean curd 白豆乾

1 tsp minced ginger

⅛ medium peeled jicama 豆薯 (60g), or 3 peeled water chestnuts 荸薺 (60g), cut into ¼-inch dice

½ tsp salt

1 tsp golden granulated sugar

¼ tsp white pepper

½ tsp Mushroom Powder 香菇粉 (page 15) or use store-bought (optional)

2 cups neutral oil, for frying

-

1 (2-inch-thick) slice winter melon 冬瓜 (600g, about 500g after seeding and peeling)

6¼ cups water

6 (1-inch) slices peeled ginger (8g to 10g)

1 tsp salt

Taiwanese basil leaves 九層塔 or Thai basil leaves (optional)

4 Slice off the green skin around the perimeter of the winter melon slice, then cut it into 1-inch chunks. Using a spoon, scrape off the seeds and any spongy tissue that surrounds them.

5 Fill a medium pot with the water and bring it to a boil over high heat. Add the ginger and winter melon and lower the heat to a slow boil. Cook, uncovered, for 30 to 40 minutes, until the winter melon is tender and translucent and a small paring knife pierces it without resistance. Add the salt and tofu balls (I usually add six to eight and save the rest) and cook for 5 minutes to allow the flavors to infuse. Taste and adjust the seasoning as needed. Transfer to a soup bowl, garnish with basil (if using), and serve. Cool any leftovers (including tofu balls) and store in an airtight container in the refrigerator for up to 3 days.

Variation: Daikon Soup

Using an equal weight of daikon radish in place of the winter melon, peel, quarter it lengthwise, and cut it into 1-inch chunks. Omit the ginger from the soup. Sprinkle a handful of chopped leaf celery and cilantro on top to finish.

鳳梨苦瓜湯 fènglí kǔguātāng | ông-lâi-khóo-kue-thng

Pineapple and Bitter Melon Soup

When cooked with pineapples, bitter melon's bitterness mellows into a savory sweetness that even kids will love. The pineapples here are no ordinary pineapples; they are fermented in soybean koji, sugar, licorice, and rice wine and are the primary flavor in this soup. The marriage between bitter melon and pineapple is usually complemented by chicken and dried fish. For the vegetarian version, I use mushrooms and fermented black soybeans. Try to find a white bitter melon if you can—it'll be less bitter. You can also add fresh tofu if you'd like an extra source of protein.

1 Rinse the fermented black soybeans once to get rid of impurities and excess salt and place them in a braising pouch or on a small piece of cheesecloth. Tie a knot to secure it and set aside.

2 Halve the bitter melon lengthwise and, using a spoon, scrape out the seeds and the surrounding pulp. (Scrape off as much of the white spongy tissue as possible—it is a source of the gourd's bitterness.) Cut on a bias into ¾-inch slices.

3 Fill a large pot with 4 cups water and bring it to a boil. Add the bitter melon and blanch it for 1 to 3 minutes to eliminate some of its bitterness (blanch it longer for older bitter melon, which has redder seeds and pulp). Drain, discard the blanching water, and set aside.

4 Rinse the large pot and dry it thoroughly. Set the pot over medium heat and add the neutral oil and ginger and cook for about 30 seconds, until fragrant. Add the shiitake and oyster mushrooms and fry for 3 to 4 minutes to release their fragrances. Add the water, the braising pouch, and the preserved pineapple with its brine and bring to a rolling boil over high heat. Lower the heat so it is still bubbling but not as rapidly and cook, uncovered, for 30 to 40 minutes, until the bitter melon has softened and the preserved pineapple has released its flavors.

5 Taste and season with salt as needed. Discard the braising pouch. Transfer the soup to a bowl or clay pot and serve. Cool any leftovers and store them in an airtight container in the refrigerator for up to 5 days.

Serves 6 to 8 as part of a spread

½ Tbsp (5g) fermented black soybeans 蔭豉/豆豉

1 small (400g) bitter melon, preferably white

3 Tbsp neutral oil

1 (1-inch) piece peeled ginger (15g), sliced

6 large fresh shiitake mushrooms (150g), stems trimmed and quartered

1 cluster oyster mushroom (100g), torn into florets (and halved if large)

8⅓ cups water

1½ cups (300g) Pineapple in Soybean Sauce 醬鳳梨 (page 50), cut into ½-inch-thick slices, plus 2 Tbsp of brine

Salt

四示申湯 sìshéntāng | sù-sîn-thng

Four Tonics Soup

Sìshéntāng is a soup that brings together four traditional Chinese tonics—dried poria, gorgon, lotus seeds, and yam. This vegetarian Taiwanese version bolsters the classic combination with Chinese pearl barley, dong quai, and cashews, bringing richness and sweetness. It's a light herbal soup that you can drink year-round and is said to provide numerous health benefits such as soothing the stomach, strengthening the spleen, and improving immunity. A-Má requests it often. A splash of dāngguījiǔ (dong quai–infused rice wine) right before serving is a must—it gives it a fragrance that makes the flavors sing.

1 To make the dong quai rice wine: Pour the rice cooking wine into a bottle with a cap. Nestle the dong quai and goji berries into the bottle. Secure the cap and let it stand at room temperature for at least overnight and preferably 1 week. Store at room temperature. Unless mold grows, there is no expiration date.

2 Pour the water into a tall pot set over high heat and bring to a boil. Add the dried poria, dried gorgon, lotus seeds, dried yam, pearl barley, female ginseng, cashews, and mushrooms. Lower the heat to medium-low or low to maintain a gentle boil and cook for 50 to 60 minutes, until the pearl barley (which takes the longest to cook) is just tender but still slightly chewy. Add the rice cooking wine and salt and cook for 5 to 10 minutes more to boil off some of the alcohol and infuse all the flavors. At the end, add a small splash of the dong quai rice wine, about 1 tablespoon. Taste and season with more salt as needed. Cool any leftovers and store in an airtight container in the refrigerator for up to 3 days.

Serves 6 to 8 as part of a spread

Dong Quai Rice Wine (makes 300ml)

1¼ cups rice cooking wine, preferably 34 percent ABV

1 piece (8g) dong quai (female ginseng)

1 Tbsp (8g) goji berries

-

8⅓ cups water

4 (2½-inch) pieces fu ling (dried poria) (60g)

¼ cup (50g) qian shi (dried gorgon)

½ cup (60g) lian zi (dried lotus seeds)

6 (2-inch) pieces huai shan (dried yam) (30g)

⅓ cup (50g) Chinese pearl barley 薏仁

1 tiny piece (1g) dong quai (female ginseng)

½ cup (70g) raw cashews

5¼ oz (150g) white shimeji mushrooms

⅓ cup rice cooking wine, preferably 34 percent ABV

2 tsp salt, plus more as needed

紅燒麵 hóngshāomiàn | âng-sio-mi
Beef Noodle Soup

Taiwan is now famous for beef noodle soup, but many Tawianese people two generations ago did not grow up eating it. My A-Má, for one, has never eaten beef in her life. As a girl, she was taught that cows and oxen were hardworking, sagacious beasts not meant for food consumption. In these earlier times, people's livelihoods depended on cows not only for heavy-duty agricultural work but also for cargo and transportation. The animals played such an important role that many considered them family. Folklore deemed only the most ungrateful farmer would slay and consume their loyal companion. Doing so would simply invite karmic retribution, so the thought of eating beef hasn't crossed her mind since.

My mom, on the other hand, is part of the generation for whom eating beef became more socially acceptable. Cows and oxen on farms were gradually replaced by tractors, their iron counterparts. And postwar, in 1949, Chinese and Muslim soldiers brought over their beef-eating habits and affinity for wheat flour noodles. When my mom was in middle school, she tried beef for the first time: a friend's mother, who was a Chinese immigrant, cooked a bowl of beef noodle soup for her.

Note: Some say Taiwanese chili bean paste came from the Sichuanese immigrants who relocated postwar to Gangshan District in Kaohsiung. They added soybeans to the original Sichuanese broad bean paste formula and adjusted it to have a sweeter taste, in accordance with the types of fermented bean pastes that the Taiwanese grew used to under Japanese rule. Try to source a similar paste such as Ming Teh brand (明德) for this soup or a Sichuan variety like Píxiàn dòubànjiàng (郫縣豆瓣醬).

Serves 4

3⅓ cups Superior Stock 上湯 (page 151)

5 cups water

6 (3-inch) pieces kombu (15g)

3 tomatoes (300g)

4 whole star anise pods (6g)

2 tsp (4g) red Sichuan peppercorns

1 whole tsaoko (Chinese black cardamom) (3g), crushed open

2 (2-inch) pieces cinnamon stick (8g)

2 tsp (5g) fennel seeds

5 whole cloves

3 pieces gan cao (dried licorice root)

2 whole dried bay leaves

1 tsp (3g) black peppercorns

3 Tbsp neutral oil

6 garlic cloves (20g), lightly smashed

1 (2-inch) piece ginger (20g), peeled and sliced

(continued)

(continued)

1 Fill a medium pot with the stock and water and bring to a boil. Remove from the heat and add the kombu. Cover to keep warm and let the kombu soak until the broth is needed.

2 Core the tomatoes and score a 1-inch X on the opposite bottom end. Bring a small saucepan of water to a rolling boil and blanch the tomatoes for 30 to 45 seconds, until the skins visibly begin to peel back. Remove the tomatoes using a slotted spoon and rinse them under cold water until cool. Peel off the skin and cut each tomato into six to eight wedges.

3 Set a large pot over medium-low heat and add the star anise, Sichuan peppercorns, tsaoko, cinnamon, fennel seeds, cloves, gan cao, dried bay leaves, and black peppercorns. Toast slowly until very fragrant but not burnt, 2 to 3 minutes. Transfer all to a braising pouch or on a small piece of cheesecloth. Tie a knot to secure and set aside.

4 In the same pot over medium-high heat, warm the neutral oil until shimmering. Add the garlic, ginger, red chilies, and scallions and quickly fry to release their fragrances, about 15 seconds. Add the yellow onions and continue to fry together until all the aromatics are browned and blistered at the edges, 2 to 3 minutes. Add the rock sugar and dòubànjiàng and fry to stain the oil and all the aromatics red, 1 to 2 minutes. Add the tomato paste and continue frying for about 1 minute to caramelize the tomato paste; its color should noticeably darken. Before anything has a chance to burn, deglaze the pot with the light soy sauce, dark soy sauce, and rice cooking wine and cook for another 1 to 2 minutes, until its fragrance has deepened slightly.

5 Remove the kombu from the reserved broth. To the pot with the soy sauce, add the broth, the braising pouch, and the lion's mane mushrooms. Bring to a rolling boil over high heat, then lower the heat to medium-low or low to maintain a slow boil, cover with a lid, and cook for 40 minutes. As the broth is cooking, you can prepare your toppings, namely the stir-fried mustard greens.

3 to 5 dried red chilies, snipped in half and seeded

3 scallions (45g), both white and green parts, cut into 1-inch segments

1 yellow onion (200g), sliced ¼ inch thick

2 tsp yellow rock sugar

2 Tbsp dòubànjiàng (chili bean paste) 豆瓣醬

1 Tbsp tomato paste

¼ cup light soy sauce

1 Tbsp dark soy sauce

¼ cup rice cooking wine

7 oz (200g) Lion's Mane Mushrooms 猴頭菇 (page 62)

Stir-Fried Mustard Greens 炒酸菜 (page 107), for serving

4 portions thick white wheat noodles (600g fresh / 300g dried)

Salt

Few heads of bok choy or vegetable of your choice

Chopped cilantro, for garnish

(continued)

6 Place a large mesh sieve over a clean pot and pour the broth through the sieve. Press on the aromatics with a ladle to extract as much of the broth as possible. Discard the cooked aromatics but keep the braising pouch. Add the braising pouch and lion's mane mushrooms back into the strained broth, along with the tomatoes. Bring the strained broth to a simmer, cover, and cook for about 10 minutes more, or until the tomatoes have just softened and released their flavors but have not turned to mush.

7 Bring a large pot of water to a gentle boil. Cook the noodles to your desired doneness and strain them into serving bowls. Add a pinch of salt to the still gently boiling water (this helps season and rid bitterness in the vegetables that will follow) and blanch the bok choy for 30 to 45 seconds, until vibrantly green and still crunchy. Add to the serving bowls. Top with the broth, lion's mane mushrooms, mustard greens, and cilantro. Serve immediately. Cool any leftovers and store in an airtight container in the refrigerator for up to 3 days.

米粉芋 mǐfěnyù | bí-hún-ōo

Taro Rice Noodle Soup

This rice noodle soup is a staple for Mid-Autumn Festival. There's a rhyming saying in Taiwanese that goes, *tsiáh bí-hún-ōo, ū hó thâu-lōo* (Eat taro rice noodle soup, get a job). The elders know their self-fulfilling prophecies. Taro is one of my favorite soup ingredients: it not only cooks to a melt-in-your-mouth tender texture but also singlehandedly brings the broth to greater savory heights. If you want a stronger taro flavor, cut some pieces into a small dice and add them to the broth; they will dissolve as you cook.

1 In a small bowl, soak the dried shiitake mushrooms in 2 cups of warm water for 20 to 25 minutes, until just tender. Drain the mushrooms but do not discard the soaking water. Snip off and discard the stems and cut the caps into thin slices. Set the mushrooms aside. Add the mushroom-soaking liquid and the remaining 6⅓ cups water to a large pot and set aside.

2 Set a wok over medium heat and heat it until it just starts smoking. Ladle in the neutral oil and swirl it around to create a nonstick surface. Add the taro and fry for 3 to 4 minutes, rotating frequently, until golden brown on all sides and it appears hardened. Using a spider strainer or slotted spoon, transfer it to a plate and set aside. Add the sliced shiitake mushrooms, green garlic, and garlic chive whites to the wok and fry together slowly for 3 to 5 minutes, until all are very fragrant and just starting to turn golden. Add the mustard greens and fry for about 1 more minute to release its fragrance. The green garlic and garlic chive whites should be just golden brown at this point. Transfer everything into the large pot with water and the mushroom soaking liquid.

3 Add the fried tofu, the corn, and the fried taro to the broth. Season with white soy sauce and salt and bring the broth to a boil. Lower the heat to medium-low or low so the broth is just slowly bubbling and

Serves 4

6 dried shiitake mushrooms (15g)

8⅓ cups water

3 Tbsp neutral oil

½ peeled taro root (300g), cut into 1- to 1½-inch chunks

1 green garlic 蒜苗 (40g), white and light green parts, cut into 1-inch segments

10 garlic chives 韭菜 (30g), white parts cut into 1-inch segments and green parts chopped and kept separate

2 oz (60g) Fermented Mustard Greens 酸菜 (page 35), preferably the core/stem portion, cut on a bias into ¼-inch-thick slices

10½ oz (300g) fried tofu

2 large ears corn (350g), husked and cut into 2-inch segments

¼ cup white soy sauce, or more salt

½ tsp salt

(continued)

(continued)

Taro Rice Noodle Soup —— continued

cook, covered, for about 30 minutes, until the taro is fuzzy looking and a paring knife inserted into the flesh goes through without resistance. Remove the taro from the soup and set aside. (The soup should taste a little salty at this point, but the rice noodles and bean sprouts will absorb some of the flavor.)

4 Add the rice noodles to the broth. Sprinkle on white pepper, mix, and boil for 1 to 2 minutes, until they reach your desired softness. Divide the noodles among serving bowls, using a pair of scissors to snip all the rice noodles in half so they are easier to eat.

5 Add the mung bean sprouts to the broth and cook until just wilted, about 30 seconds. Add the sprouts to the serving bowls.

6 Add the taro back to the broth until heated through, taking care not to stir too much as the taro can now break. Divide the taro, corn, and fried tofu among the serving bowls. Ladle the broth into the bowls and top each bowl with leaf celery, garlic chive greens, cilantro (if using), and fried shallots. Serve immediately, with extra white pepper on the side. Cool any leftovers and store in an airtight container in the refrigerator for up to 3 days.

1 bundle (about 100g) dried thin Taiwanese rice noodles 細炊粉

¼ tsp white pepper, plus more for serving

3½ oz (100g) mung bean sprouts

2 stalks leaf celery 芹菜 (40g), no leaves, finely chopped

Chopped cilantro, for garnish (optional)

4 tsp (20g) Fried Shallots 油蔥 (page 175)

麵線羹 miànxiàngēng | 麵線糊 mī-suànn-kôo
Mee Sua

A starch-thickened soup (gēng) always has a spot on Taiwanese tables. It stays hot for a long time and can extend a little food for a lot of people. Mee sua is made with chewy red vermicelli and, like most gēng soups, gets its signature flavor from a splash of Taiwanese black vinegar. One pot makes a wholesome family meal. Serve it with pureed raw garlic, vegetarian sha-cha sauce, chili oil, and chopped cilantro.

1 In a small bowl, soak the dried shiitake mushrooms in 2 cups of warm water for 20 to 30 minutes, until fully soft. Snip off and discard the stems and cut the caps into thin batons. Set aside the mushrooms and their soaking liquid separately.

2 Rinse the red vermicelli three to five times to rid it of excess salt. Drain and use scissors to snip the vermicelli into 2- to 2½-inch segments.

3 Add the mushroom-soaking liquid and 6⅓ cups of the water to a large pot. Bring to a boil over high heat and add the shiitake mushroom batons, wood ear fungus, bamboo shoots, enoki mushrooms, carrots, and fried shallots. Lower the heat to medium or medium-low so the broth is just gently boiling and cook for 10 minutes. Add the vermicelli and, once the broth is back to a boil, cook for 7 to 10 minutes to soften the vermicelli.

4 Meanwhile, in a small bowl, make a thin slurry with the sweet potato starch and the remaining ½ cup water. Mix until no lumps remain.

5 To the large pot, mix in the sugar, light soy sauce, salt, white pepper, and black vinegar. Drizzle in the sweet potato starch slurry, stirring vigorously to incorporate. Add the sesame oil to finish. Taste and adjust the seasoning as needed. Serve immediately, with your desired toppings on the side. Cool any leftovers and store in an airtight container in the refrigerator for up to 3 days.

Serves 4 to 6

12 (30g) dried shiitake mushrooms

8⅓ cups plus ½ cup water

7 oz (200g) Taiwanese red vermicelli 紅麵線

3½ oz (100g) fresh wood ear fungus 木耳, cut into thin batons

3½ oz (100g) shelled, cooked bamboo shoots, cut into thin batons

3½ oz (100g) enoki mushrooms, cut into 2-inch segments

1 oz (30g) carrots, cut into thin batons

4 tsp (20g) Fried Shallots 油蔥 (page 175)

¼ cup (32g) fine sweet potato starch

1½ Tbsp golden granulated sugar

2½ Tbsp light soy sauce

1 tsp salt

½ tsp white pepper

3½ Tbsp Taiwanese black vinegar 烏醋

½ tsp sesame oil 香油

Mains

"See, my ancestors were smart." My mom smirked. "They were one of the few hundred Dutch who boarded the ship to Taiwan. You're lucky to marry a smart woman like me," she said to my dad, holding up her chin proudly. "Let's not rush to conclusions," my dad said, curling his lips back at her. "Who knows, maybe they were the janitors on the ship!"

At this point in the book, it feels like a travesty not to talk more about my maternal grandma, whom I call A-Má. Although I never lived with my maternal family, they represent an immigrant experience that feels important to me and my quest to bring Taiwanese food abroad. A-Má was born in Kaohsiung, in southern Taiwan, to a wūyúzi (cured mullet roe) maker of Dutch descent. She grew up in a Buddhist household and never ate beef. After she married my maternal grandpa, a traditional Chinese medicine (TCM) practitioner and soldier who fled from Fuzhou after the Chinese civil war, they emigrated to Maryland. In their new home, she raised my mom and her three other children and cooked the Taiwanese meals she remembered, using ingredients found in American grocery stores.

A-Má carried with her a hardcover cookbook enshrined with the letters *PEI MEI*, for celebrity chef Fù Péiméi 傅培梅. Fù hosted Taiwan's first cooking show, which aired in 1962, a time when the melding of Chinese and Taiwanese cuisines and people both enriched and complicated what it meant to be Taiwanese. The show called back to a time when young, newlywed women like my A-Má didn't have a chance to formally learn how to cook. But Fù, with few words and a swift cleaver, demonstrated how easy it was to whip up a meal in a matter of minutes. A-Má didn't just watch her shows; she attended in-person classes at her cooking school. Fù often said the reason she took on cooking was simply to please her husband. A-Má resonated with her story, driven by the want to relive her own Chinese husband's childhood tastes. By the time Fù's shows and cookbooks reached the world, A-Má had become a very skilled cook. The meals she'd cook on a regular weekend, as my mom would describe, rivaled the spreads at a *pān-toh* (Taiwanese roadside banquet).

I've spent a lot of time trying to define what it means for food to be Taiwanese and whether my vegetarian food could truly fit into that definition. A-Má's story makes me think that my desire to forcibly anchor myself to something is rather pointless. Maybe there isn't a single definition. Everyone has their own definitions, and when we sit down to listen to those of others, the world is a more empathetic and delicious place.

Cooking Rice

Once I asked my A-Má why she always made the same few dishes. She answered firmly, "It must be very xiàfàn [good with rice] to get the kids to eat more nutrients!" It's warming to hear a response so simple and motherly. A-Má and I are the same kind of people. We can't go through a meal without eating some form of rice.

A-Má taught my mom how she cooked rice, and my mom in turn taught me. When I first started cooking for myself, I lived with my brother in the United States. It was a routine that brought me back to Taiwan. Each afternoon, when the sunlight started to dim, I headed over to the pantry cabinet and dragged out a heavy bag of white rice. I scooped the rice cup into the quicksand of grains and lifted out a pretty mound. I dumped the rice into the stainless-steel pot and swooshed them around under running water as they collided between my fingers like tiny marbles. I knew to wash them at least three times and to measure the proportions with a perpendicular finger. "The rice comes up to the first knuckle," I recited my mom's words in my head, "and the water to the second. That makes the rice-to-water ratio one to one." I then flipped the rice cooker's lid upside down and filled it with water, as my mom would, and tipped it into the machine until it just covered the steam holes.

It's odd that something as mundane as a bowl of rice could take me thousands of miles back home. Each time I lift the lid, the fragrant steam of cooked rice whirls into my nostrils and fills my heart with a feeling of nourishment unlike anything else. When my brother and I eat together and he goes to the rice cooker to scoop a second bowl, I wonder what kind of smile it would put on A-Má's wrinkly face.

素滷飯 sùlǔfàn | sòo-lóo-pn̄g

Braised Pork over Rice

The recipe that follows was made with my mom's braised pork in mind. Whenever she cooked it, she'd make a huge pot, and we'd eat from it for as many consecutive days as it took for us to finish it. When we got tired of eating it over rice, we used it to dress different vegetables. Her braised pork is simple and as homestyle as can be. Soy sauce is the main seasoning; rock sugar plays a balancing act. Fried shallots permeate throughout, and so does mushroom umami. Five-spice is necessary but cannot be overpowering. The flavors are bold and complex, yet never drown out subtleties of that freshly steamed bowl of rice.

In place of the two gluten products, I'll sometimes use a mixture of fresh and fried tofu, or crumble tempeh. To keep this and any other dish that needs fried shallots allium-free, fry shredded green cabbage, shredded burdock root, or a mixture of chopped cilantro and celery in sesame oil to substitute.

1 In a small bowl, soak the gluten threads in 2 cups hot water, changing the water when it cools, for about 1 hour, until soft and pliable. Drain, rinse, and finely mince the gluten threads. Set aside.

2 In another small bowl, soak the dried shiitake mushrooms in the warm stock for 20 to 30 minutes, until fully soft. Drain the mushrooms, reserving the stock. Snip off and discard the stems and cut the caps into ¾-inch chunks. Set the mushrooms and stock aside separately.

3 Set a wok over medium heat and heat it until it just starts smoking. Ladle in the neutral oil and swirl it around to create a nonstick surface. Add the garlic and cook for 15 to 30 seconds, until fragrant. Add the diced gluten intestine and fry for about 2 minutes, until just starting to turn golden. Add the mushrooms and fry for 2 minutes to release their fragrance. Add the sugar, star anise, bay leaf, and gluten threads. Swirl

Serves 6 to 8 as part of a spread

2 Gluten Threads 皮絲 (page 59), or use store-bought (50g total)

10 dried shiitake mushrooms (25g)

2 cups warm All-Purpose Stock 高湯 (page 150) or water, plus more as needed

3 Tbsp neutral oil

5 garlic cloves or 1 (2-inch) piece peeled ginger, minced

1 Gluten Intestine 麵腸 (page 58) or use store-bought (100g total), cut into ½-inch dice

2 tsp (10g) yellow rock sugar

2 whole star anise pods

1 whole dried bay leaf

2 Tbsp light soy sauce

2 Tbsp Taiwanese rice cooking wine

2 Tbsp (30g) Fried Shallots 油蔥 (recipe follows), or use store-bought

(continued)

(continued)

in the soy sauce and fry the pieces in it for about 1 minute, until the fragrance has deepened. Follow with the rice cooking wine and, once fragrant, add the fried shallots and mushroom-soaking stock. Adjust the heat to high and bring everything to a rolling boil. Season with the salt, white pepper, and five-spice. Lower the heat to a slow boil and braise, uncovered, for 8 to 10 minutes, until the sauce is reduced by about half.

4 Remove the wok from the heat, cover, and let sit for at least 30 minutes before serving to allow the flavors to infuse without overcooking the gluten. Taste and add more salt as needed.

5 Ladle over steaming hot rice and top with the cucumbers. Serve immediately. Cool any leftovers and store them in airtight containers in the refrigerator for up to 1 week.

1 tsp salt, plus more as needed

¼ tsp white pepper

¼ tsp Five-Spice 五香粉 (page 27) or use store-bought

Steamed rice, for serving

Cucumbers in Sweet Soy Sauce 醬瓜 (page 47) or use store-bought, for serving

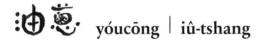 **yóucōng** | **iû-tshang**

Fried Shallots

1 Peel the shallots and cut lengthwise into very thin slices, each about 1/16 inch thick. Cut as evenly as possible so they will cook uniformly.

2 Set a wok over medium-low heat and add the neutral oil and sliced shallots. Slowly and steadily fry the shallots, stirring occasionally, for 15 to 20 minutes. When all the shallots just turn golden, remove them from the oil with a spider strainer and spread them out on a baking tray in a single layer to cool. The shallots will darken more as they cool; don't overshoot it or they'll taste burnt. Scoop the fried shallots into a lidded 2-cup glass container. Fill the container with the shallot frying oil, then secure the lid. Store in the refrigerator for up to 6 months.

Makes one 2-cup jar

8 oz (225 g) shallots, preferably small Asian shallots

1 cup neutral oil

梅乾菜素燥 méigāncài sùzào

Minced Pork with Aged Mustard Greens

Aside from xiāngchūn, or Chinese toon (*Toona sinensis*), Buddhist vegetarians often employ the aromatic qualities of méigāncài (aged mustard greens, see page 35) to make their allium-free equivalent of braised or minced pork. Both the textured vegetable protein (TVP) and méigāncài are highly absorbent of oil, hence, the higher-than-normal amount of oil called for in this recipe. Oil is crucial for bringing richness and balance to our otherwise fatless vegetable protein mince. Frying the mince in oil is also an integral step in developing a desirable firm texture.

1 Gently rinse the mustard greens. In a medium bowl, soak the greens in 3 cups water for about 1 hour, until they become pliable. Carefully rinse between the leaves and swoosh the greens around in the water to remove any trapped sand. Empty and refill the same bowl with 3 more cups water and soak for 4 to 5 more hours, changing the water once more halfway through. The water should go from opaque brown to clear. Wring the mustard dry, then chop it into a fine mince. The leaves can get tangled; chop them through a few more times so they won't be in long strands. Set aside.

2 In a medium bowl, soak the dried shiitake mushrooms in the warm water for 20 to 30 minutes, until fully soft. Drain the mushrooms, reserving the soaking liquid. Snip off and discard the stems and chop the caps into a fine mince (about the size of the TVP). Set the mushrooms and their soaking liquid aside separately.

3 In a small bowl, soak the TVP in hot water to cover for about 10 minutes, until springy and expanded. Drain into a sieve. Rinse and squeeze the TVP until its liquid runs clear.

Serves 6 to 8 as part of a spread

1 bundle aged mustard greens 梅乾菜 (50g, about 100g after rehydrating)

8 dried shiitake mushrooms (20g)

3⅓ cups warm water

½ cup (56g) textured vegetable protein (TVP) mince 素肉丁

½ cup neutral oil

1 Tbsp peeled and minced fresh ginger

¼ cup light soy sauce

2 pieces (40g) Oriental Pickling Melons in White Soy Sauce 蔭瓜 (page 49), finely minced (optional)

1 Tbsp golden granulated sugar 二砂糖, plus more as needed

2 whole star anise pods (2g)

1 tsp salt

¼ tsp black pepper

(continued)

(continued)

Minced Pork with Aged Mustard Greens —— continued

4 Heat a wok over medium heat until just smoking. Ladle in the neutral oil and swirl it around to create a nonstick surface. Add the TVP and fry for 5 to 8 minutes, until the steam dissipates and the TVP browns a little. Push the TVP to the side, add the ginger where the oil pools, and fry for 15 to 30 seconds, until the ginger is fragrant. Add the mushrooms and fry for 2 to 3 minutes to release their fragrance. Swirl in the soy sauce, then add the oriental pickling melons (if using), sugar, and star anise. Fry everything together for about 1 minute, until the fragrance of the soy sauce has deepened. Add the aged mustard greens and stir-fry briefly, until you start to smell their fragrance. (Don't stir-fry the mustard for too long, as it is prone to burning.) Add the reserved mushroom-soaking liquid. Adjust the heat to high and bring to a rolling boil. Season with salt, cover partially, and braise for 40 to 45 minutes. Finish with black pepper and adjust the seasonings if necessary.

5 Ladle over steaming hot rice and serve immediately, alongside the braised bamboo shoots and blanched vegetables and soup of your choosing.

Steamed rice, for serving

Braised Bamboo Shoots (recipe follows) and blanched vegetables (see page 135) and soup (see page 146) of your choosing, for serving

筍絲 sǔnsī | sún-si

Braised Bamboo Shoots

Few side dishes remind me of *kóo-tsá-bī* (old-time flavors) more than this one. Preserved bamboo shoots are musky and sour in the most attractive way possible, and packed to the brim with umami. In Taiwan, it isn't uncommon to see the shoots braised with preserved vegetables such as fúcài (preserved mustard greens, see page 41), but I like the original taste.

1 Rinse the preserved bamboo shoots three or four times, until the water turns from a murky yellow to a faint off-white. In a medium bowl, soak the bamboo shoots in water to cover for 15 to 20 minutes. Drain and set the preserved bamboo shoots aside.

2 Bring a medium pot with 4 cups water to a rolling boil. Add the preserved bamboo shoots. Lower the heat so the water is still boiling but not as rapidly and boil for 15 minutes. Drain and rinse with water until cool to the touch.

3 In a small pot over medium heat, warm the neutral oil. Add the garlic cloves and fry 3 to 4 minutes to caramelize the cloves on all sides. Add the prepared bamboo shoots and stir-fry for a few more seconds to release some fragrance. Add the stock all at once. Bring everything to a rolling boil, then reduce the heat to medium-low or low to maintain a gentler one. Cover partially with a lid and simmer for about 30 minutes, or until the broth has reduced by about half and all the bamboo shoots (especially the thicker parts) are tender, crunchy, and not at all rubbery.

4 Transfer to a plate and serve immediately. Cool any leftovers and store in an airtight container in the refrigerator for up to 1 week.

Serves 4 to 6 as a side

7 oz (200g) preserved bamboo shoots 筍茸, preferably made from ma bamboo shoots 麻竹筍

1 Tbsp neutral oil

5 garlic cloves

2½ cups All-Purpose Stock 高湯 (page 150) or water

紅麴炒飯 hóngqú chǎofàn | âng-khak-tshá-pn̄g

Red Yeast Fried Rice

This isn't a Taiwanese cookbook without fried rice; on this island we treat the dish as though a form of art. The pinkish color and distinctive flavor of this fried rice come from hóngzāo, a savory by-product from brewing alcohol using hóngqú (red koji) inoculated rice. I tend to keep this fried rice lightly seasoned so it can act as a bed for other accompanying dishes. If you want a stronger flavor, add a small scoop of dòubànjiàng (chili bean paste) or a splash of light soy sauce as you fry. Serve with chǎosuāncài (Stir-Fried Mustard Greens, page 107) for a street-stall experience.

Serves 4 as part of a spread

1½ oz (40g) Preserved Radish 菜脯 (page 42)

3 Tbsp neutral oil

14 oz (400g) cooked white rice, refrigerated overnight

4 tsp red yeast sauce 紅糟

3½ oz (100g) leafy greens, such as bok choy, green cabbage, or a mix, chopped into a roughly ½-inch dice

¼ tsp white pepper

1 Rinse the preserved radishes for a few seconds to rid them of any dust and wring them dry by hand. Chop them into a fine mince, and rinse once more very quickly to get rid of any excess salt. Drain well.

2 Heat a wok over maximum heat until just smoking. Ladle in the neutral oil and swirl it around to create a nonstick surface. Add the minced radish and cook for 3 to 5 seconds, until fragrant. Add the rice. Using the back of the wok ladle, gently press on the rice to separate the individual grains so they heat evenly. You want to exert some pressure but not so much that you squish the rice.

3 Continue heating the rice while pressing and tossing it constantly. You should start to smell its fragrance and hear popping sounds. When the grains become mostly distinct, drizzle in the red yeast sauce. Quickly toss the rice to evenly distribute the color and follow with the leafy greens. Continue tossing until the greens are just wilted, 30 to 45 seconds. Sprinkle with the white pepper. Ladle onto a serving plate and serve immediately. Cool any leftovers and store them in an airtight container in the refrigerator for up to 1 week.

咖哩飯 gālǐfàn | ka-lí-pn̄g

Curry Rice

Like in Japan, curry in Taiwan has Western roots. Japanese curry is served at Bolero, the first Western diner in Taiwan, where my parents went for special occasions. My mom used Japanese roux cubes to make us the same curry growing up, and to this day, its flavor is still welded to my palate. I make my Taiwanese-style Japanese curry from powder and thicken it with blended peanuts and cashews. You get an additional dimension of flavor, which is needed in a vegetarian recipe, and you won't need to add flour in roux cubes or a starch slurry. The secret ingredients in my curry are light soy sauce, ketchup, and cocoa powder—each gives a background boost of umami, complexity, or richness.

1 In a medium bowl, soak the dried shiitake mushrooms in the warm water for 20 to 30 minutes, until fully soft. Drain the mushrooms, reserving the liquid. Snip off and discard the stems and halve any especially large mushroom caps. Set the mushrooms and their soaking liquid aside separately.

2 Preheat the oven to 355°F (180°C). Spread the peanuts and cashews in a single layer on a baking tray. Roast for about 15 minutes, occasionally stirring, until golden brown and nutty smelling. Set aside to cool.

3 In a blender, blend the cooled nuts, apple, and 1 cup of the mushroom soaking liquid for 2 to 3 minutes into a slurry that is as smooth as possible. Set aside.

4 In a wok or Dutch oven over medium-high heat, warm the neutral oil. Add the onions and cook, constantly stirring for 4 to 6 minutes, until thoroughly browned. Add the garlic (if using) and curry powder and fry the curry powder in the oil for about 30 seconds, until fragrant. Add the potatoes, lion's mane mushrooms, shiitake mushrooms, the remaining soaking liquid, and the blended nut mixture. Season with salt, mix

Serves 4 to 6 as part of a spread

6 medium dried shiitake mushrooms (15g)

2½ cups warm water, plus more as necessary

2 Tbsp (25g) unsalted raw, shelled peanuts

¼ cup (35g) unsalted raw cashews

½ peeled apple (50g), roughly chopped

2 Tbsp neutral oil

½ yellow onion (100g), roughly diced

2 garlic cloves, minced (optional)

1 Tbsp (8g) curry powder, preferably S&B brand Golden Curry

1 large peeled russet potato (200g), cut into 1-inch chunks

3½ oz (100g) Lion's Mane Mushrooms 猴頭菇 (page 62)

1 tsp salt

½ carrot (50g), cut into ½-inch cubes

well, and bring to a gentle boil. Simmer for 15 to 20 minutes, until the curry gradually thickens and the potatoes are just tender with a slight resistance when pierced with a paring knife. Add the carrots, light soy sauce, sugar, ketchup, white pepper, black pepper, and cocoa powder. Simmer for about 5 minutes more, to infuse all the flavors and soften the carrots. Taste and adjust the seasoning as needed.

5 Serve immediately over a bed of freshly steamed rice. Cool any leftovers and store in an airtight container in the refrigerator for up to 3 days.

2 tsp light soy sauce

1 tsp golden granulated sugar

2 tsp ketchup

¼ tsp white pepper

¼ tsp black pepper

½ tsp pure cocoa powder

Steamed rice, for serving

高麗菜飯 gāolìcài fàn | ko-lê-tshài-pīg

Cabbage Rice

Taiwan is proudly second in the world in annual cabbage consumption per capita. Beside stir-fried cabbage and hot pot, I'd say that this is the dish that tipped the scale. Braising cabbage and carrots renders them crunchy tender and sweet. I make this like yóufàn (Taiwanese Sticky Rice, page 220)—mixing in cooked rice instead of starting from raw—to get distinct moist yet chewy grains. Serve with clear soup.

1 Rinse the white rice three to five times, until the water runs mostly clear. Drain well and place it in the inner pot of a rice cooker. Cook with a roughly 1 : 0.8 rice-to-water ratio to yield a slightly dry rice.

2 Dig your thumb into the top center of the gluten intestine and pry it open to reveal its layers. Work downward until you have a whole, flat sheet of gluten with lots of exposed nooks and crannies. Chop into a fine mince and set aside.

3 Heat a wok over medium-high heat until just smoking. Ladle in the neutral oil and swirl it around to create a nonstick surface. Add the gluten intestine and fry for 1 to 2 minutes, until crisp and lightly golden. Swirl in the light soy sauce. Add the garlic, scallion whites, and carrots and fry for 5 to 10 seconds, until fragrant. Add the green cabbage and salt and stir-fry for 2 to 3 minutes. You don't need to be too timid with the heat—a little charring is very tasty here. Add the stock and fried shallots and bring to a boil over high heat. Cook for 8 to 10 minutes, until the broth is mostly evaporated.

4 Turn off the heat and scoop in the hot steamed rice. With a spatula, use a shoveling motion to mix the rice evenly, coating every grain with the sauce. Dust with the white pepper. Transfer the cabbage rice to bowls and serve immediately. Cool any leftovers and store in an airtight container in the refrigerator for up to 3 days.

Serves 6 to 8 as part of a spread

1½ cups (360g) short-grain white rice

1 Gluten Intestine 麵腸 (page 58) or use store-bought (100g)

2 Tbsp neutral oil

1 tsp light soy sauce

6 garlic cloves, each cut into 2 or 3 slices

1 scallion, white and green parts separated and chopped

¼ carrot (50g), cut into thin batons

½ head green cabbage (400g), cut or torn into 2-inch pieces

½ tsp salt, plus more as needed

1 cup All-Purpose Stock 高湯 (page 150) or water

4 tsp (20g) Fried Shallots 油蔥 (page 175)

¼ tsp white pepper, plus more as needed

菜脯蛋 tshài-póo-nn̄g

Preserved Radish Omelet

This is a Buddhist vegetarian version of a homestyle omelet that A-Gong used to make. If it met his standards, he'd say it "tasted of meat." It didn't actually contain any, but with the crunchy tender, savory preserved radishes dotted throughout the omelet, it resembled the flavor and texture of meat. Tofu skin paste is a paste made from stirring together still-wet fresh tofu skin, as soon as they're lifted from hot soy milk. If you can't find it, you can also use an equal weight of a plant-based scramble or four large eggs. I make another version with regular tofu skin rolls, but rather than forming it like an omelet, I open the rolls up and stir-fry them with the preserved radish like large sheets of scrambled eggs.

Serves 1

2 oz (60g) Preserved Radish 菜脯 (page 42)

7 oz (200g) tofu skin paste 豆包漿

1 small bunch (5g to 8g) Taiwanese basil leaves 九層塔 or Thai basil leaves, roughly chopped

¼ tsp white pepper

1 tsp neutral oil

1 Rinse the preserved radish for a few seconds to get rid of any dust, wring it dry, and chop into a ¼-inch mince. Rinse the mince once more very quickly to wash off any excess salt. Drain and set aside.

2 Heat a small (preferably 9-inch) nonstick pan over medium to medium-high heat until warm. Add the radish and stir-fry for 1 to 2 minutes, until very fragrant. Transfer to a large bowl. Add the tofu skin paste, basil, and white pepper and mix well.

3 In the same nonstick pan over medium heat, warm the neutral oil. Add the paste to the pan and flatten it into a rough circle about ¼ inch thick. Fry slowly for 5 to 7 minutes, pressing with a spatula to ensure even cooking. Once this side of the omelet feels set and easily moves around the pan, place a plate over the omelet and quickly but carefully invert the whole pan and flip the omelet onto the plate. Slide the omelet back into the pan and cook the other side for 5 to 7 minutes more, until it's golden. Transfer to a serving plate and serve immediately. Cool any leftovers and store them in an airtight container in the refrigerator for up to 2 days.

蔭豉豆腐 yìnchǐ dòufǔ | ìm-sīnn-tāu-hū

Black Bean Tofu

Yìnchǐ (fermented black soybeans) is an important Taiwanese flavor. To make them, black soybeans are steamed until fully cooked, injected with koji, salted, and fermented for months, resulting in a deeply earthy taste that is full of umami. Yìnchǐ's flavor goes perfectly with the tartness and sweetness of pickled cordia seeds (seeds of the *Cordia dichotoma* tree, preserved in soy sauce). This is one of my favorites to eat with rice; remember to serve with a piping hot bowl!

1 In a small bowl, soak the dried shiitake mushrooms in the warm stock for 20 to 25 minutes, until just tender. Drain the mushrooms, reserving the soaking liquid. Snip off and discard the stems and finely mince the caps. Set the mushrooms and their soaking liquid aside separately.

2 In a small bowl, soak the TVP in hot water to cover for about 10 minutes, until springy and enlarged. Drain it through a sieve and squeeze out any excess liquid. The liquid will be a little yellow. Continue to rinse and squeeze the TVP until the liquid runs clear to get rid of any undesired soy flavors.

3 Rinse the fermented black soybeans once to wash off impurities and excess salt. Drain and set aside.

4 In a wok over high heat, bring 4 cups of the water and ½ tsp salt to a rolling boil. Lower the heat to medium so the water is still bubbling but not as rapidly. Add the tofu and blanch for 2 minutes. Using a spider strainer or slotted spoon, transfer the tofu to a plate and set aside.

5 Rinse the wok and set it over medium-high heat until just smoking. Ladle in the neutral oil and swirl it around to create a nonstick surface. Add the TVP and fry for 3 to 6 minutes, until the steam dissipates and the TVP becomes a little golden. Push the TVP to the side and add the ginger and green garlic whites in the center of the wok for about

Serves 4 to 6 as part of a spread

4 dried shiitake mushrooms (10g)

1¼ cups warm All-Purpose Stock 高湯 (page 150) or water

1½ Tbsp (10g) textured vegetable protein mince (TVP) 素肉丁

1½ Tbsp (15g) fermented black soybeans 蔭豉/豆豉

4 cups plus 1 Tbsp water

Salt

1 (300g) block soft or silken tofu, cut into ¾-inch cubes

2 Tbsp neutral oil

2 tsp minced ginger

2 green garlic 蒜苗 (80g), white and light green parts separated from the greens, all cut into ¾-inch segments

1 Tbsp (15g) pickled cordia seeds 破布子, cored

1 tsp golden granulated sugar

(continued)   (continued)

Black Bean Tofu —— continued

30 seconds, stirring, until fragrant. Add the mushrooms and stir-fry for 1 to 2 minutes to release their fragrance. Add the fermented black soybeans, pickled cordia seeds, sugar, and soy sauce paste and toss together a few times to combine. Swirl in the rice cooking wine down the sides and add the mushroom-soaking liquid to the wok. Bring to a gentle boil, carefully slide in the tofu along with any liquid that has seeped out, and cook for 4 to 6 minutes to infuse all the flavors.

6 Meanwhile, in a small bowl, make a slurry with the potato starch and the remaining 1 Tbsp water. Mix until no lumps remain.

7 Add the chili rings and garlic greens to the wok, then drizzle in the slurry. Gently swirl the wok around without using a spatula (the tofu is fragile) until the sauce thickens. Finish with the sesame oil and white pepper. Taste and season with salt if needed. Transfer to a serving dish and serve immediately. Cool any leftovers and store in an airtight container in the refrigerator for up to 5 days.

2 Tbsp soy sauce paste 醬油膏

1 Tbsp Taiwanese rice cooking wine

1 tsp potato starch 太白粉 or cornstarch

1 fresh red chili, cut into thin rings

1 tsp sesame oil 香油

Pinch of white pepper

白菜滷 **báicàilǔ** | **pėh-tshài-lóo**

Napa Cabbage Stew

I never got to attend a traditional *pān-toh* (Taiwanese roadside banquet), but I experienced it through the old-time movies and dramas that A-Gong would watch. This dish, along with *wǔliǔjū* (Five Willow Fried Fish, page 197), is among the most defining *pān-toh* foods. Perhaps people love them because they are just as good for home cooking as for an extravagant banquet table. Stewing the napa cabbage releases a rich umami sweetness, which is complemented by the savory flavors and biǎnyú (扁魚, dried flounder) taste of sha-cha sauce. If you can, use a bāoxīn (包心, "green cabbage resembling") variety of napa cabbage that is slightly rounder than average, because it retains a delicate crunch even after cooking for a long time.

1 In a small bowl, soak the dried shiitake mushrooms in the warm stock for 20 to 25 minutes, until just tender. Drain the mushrooms, reserving the soaking liquid. Snip off and discard the stems and cut the caps into thin slices. Set the mushrooms and their soaking liquid aside separately.

2 In a medium bowl, soak the cellophane noodles in room temperature water to cover for 10 minutes to rehydrate them. If the noodles are long, snip them in half with scissors so they are easier to eat. Drain and set aside.

3 Bring a wok with 4 cups water to a boil over medium-high heat. Blanch the napa cabbage for about 30 seconds, until just wilted. Using a spider strainer or slotted spoon, transfer to a plate and set aside. Drain and rinse the wok.

4 Set the wok over medium heat and ladle in the neutral oil. Swirl the oil around to create a nonstick surface. Add the enoki mushrooms and fry for 4 to 6 minutes, until very fragrant, golden brown, and crisp. Using a spider strainer or slotted spoon, transfer the mushrooms to a plate and

Serves 6 to 8 as part of a spread

4 dried shiitake mushrooms (10g)

3 cups warm All-Purpose Stock 高湯 (page 150)

1 bundle (40g to 50g) cellophane noodles 冬粉

1 small head (600g) napa cabbage, cut into 2-inch pieces

½ cup neutral oil, for frying

3½ oz (100g) enoki mushrooms, cut into ¾-inch segments and separated

3½ oz (100g) fresh tofu skin rolls 豆包

5 garlic cloves, lightly crushed

2 scallions, white and light green parts only, cut into 1-inch segments

1 (1-inch) chunk carrot (30g), cut into thin batons

1 tsp soybean paste nonspicy dòubànjiàng 豆瓣醬

(continued)

(continued)

Napa Cabbage Stew —— continued

set aside. Add the tofu skin rolls to the wok and fry for about 1 minute on each side, until golden and puffed. Using a spider strainer or slotted spoon, transfer to a cutting board and tear or slice them into 1½-inch-wide strips.

5 Pour out all but 2 Tbsp of the oil and heat the wok over medium heat. Add the garlic and scallions and fry for 15 to 30 seconds, until fragrant. Add the shiitake mushrooms and carrots, tossing to combine. Add the soybean paste and fry for 1 to 2 minutes to release all the fragrances. Add the napa cabbage and swirl in the rice cooking wine. Using a fine-mesh sieve, strain the mushroom-soaking stock into the wok. Bring to a boil, season with the salt and sugar, and braise, uncovered, on a slow boil for 4 to 5 minutes to soften the cabbage and concentrate all the flavors.

6 Meanwhile, in a small bowl, make a slurry with the potato starch and the water. Mix until no lumps remain.

7 Add the sha-cha sauce, wood ear, cellophane noodles, fried tofu skin, and the fried enoki mushrooms to the wok and cook for 2 to 3 minutes. Stir in the potato starch slurry to just slightly thicken the stew. Taste and add more salt or sugar as needed. Sprinkle in white pepper and drizzle on the sesame oil. Give everything a final mix, ladle it into a serving bowl or clay pot, and serve immediately. Cool any leftovers and store them in an airtight container in the refrigerator for up to 3 days.

1 Tbsp Taiwanese rice cooking wine

1½ tsp salt, plus more as needed

½ tsp sugar, plus more as needed

½ tsp potato starch 太白粉 or cornstarch

1 Tbsp water

2 Tbsp vegetarian sha-cha ("barbecue") sauce 素沙茶醬, preferably Bull Head brand 牛頭牌

2 oz (60g) fresh wood ear fungus 木耳, torn into 1½-inch pieces

¼ tsp white pepper

1 tsp sesame oil 香油

三杯猴頭菇 sānbēi hóutóugū
Three Cup Lion's Mane Mushrooms

Sānbēi (three cups) refers to the three essential condiments used in this dish: toasted sesame oil, soy sauce, and rice cooking wine. I've always taken the name quite literally, using equal parts of the three. This is a sauce that can go with just about anything, so don't feel restricted to lion's mane mushrooms. To name a few, tofu, dòujī (Soy Chicken, page 61), miàncháng (Gluten Intestine, page 58), king oyster mushrooms, zǐcàigāo (Purple Laver Cake, page 115), and huángdìdòu (lima beans) are all good options. Use neutral oil to panfry whichever one you choose until golden-brown before tossing it with the sesame oil and ginger.

Heat a wok over medium-high heat until just smoking. Turn off the heat, ladle in the toasted sesame oil and swirl it around to create a nonstick surface. Turn down the heat to medium. (Be conservative with the heat. Toasted sesame oil tends to taste bitter when overheated.) Add the ginger and slowly sizzle for 7 to 10 minutes, until they are blistered, dry looking, and curled. Add the lion's mane mushrooms and toss a few times to coat them in the sesame oil and ginger. Add the sugar, swirl in the light soy sauce and rice cooking wine, and stir-fry for a few seconds to glaze all the pieces. Add the water and bring to a boil. Lower the heat so the sauce is still bubbling but not as rapidly and cook for about 15 minutes to allow the mushrooms to soak up all the flavors and the sauce to reduce by about three-quarters. Remove from the heat and add the sliced chilies and basil leaves, tossing to combine. Transfer to a serving dish and serve immediately. Cool any leftovers and store in an airtight container in the refrigerator for up to 3 days.

Serves 4 as part of a spread

2 Tbsp toasted sesame oil 麻油, preferably toasted black sesame oil 黑麻油

2 (1½-inch) pieces unpeeled ginger (20g), thinly sliced

10½ oz (300g) Lion's Mane Mushrooms 猴頭菇 (page 62)

1 Tbsp golden granulated sugar

2 Tbsp light soy sauce

2 Tbsp Taiwanese rice cooking wine

1 cup water

1 fresh red chili (about 10g), sliced on a bias

1 bunch Taiwanese basil 九層塔 (20g) or Thai basil

金瓜米粉炒 jīnguā mǐfěnchǎo | kim-kue bí-hún-tshá

Pumpkin Fried Rice Noodles

Sometimes I eat fried *bí-hún* (Taiwanese rice noodles), and it returns the memory I have of slurping it piping hot out of a plastic box in the back of my mom's car. It's as if I could once again feel the steam of toasted rice and fried shallots that thickened the air in that little space. If your rice noodles are thin as strands of hair, they can be added directly to the wok. For slightly thicker noodles, blanch them in boiling water for 10 seconds, until they turn white, before using them in this recipe. See the photograph on page 170.

1 In a small bowl, soak the dried shiitake mushrooms in the warm water for 20 to 25 minutes, until soft. Drain the mushrooms, reserving the soaking water. Snip off and discard the stems and cut the caps into thin slices. Set the mushrooms and their soaking liquid aside separately.

2 Heat a wok over high heat until just smoking. Ladle in the neutral oil and swirl it around to create a nonstick surface. Add the scallion whites and shiitake mushrooms and stir-fry for 20 to 30 seconds to release their fragrances. Add the carrots, onion, green cabbage, and pumpkin and stir-fry for 1 minute. Swirl in the light soy sauce and add the mushroom-soaking liquid. Season with the salt and fried shallots. Bring to a boil and cook for about 5 minutes, until the pumpkin is just tender and easily breaks in half when poked with a chopstick.

3 Add the rice noodles to the wok. Using one chopstick in each hand, lift and toss the noodles in the broth, as if you're untangling a bowl of noodles that sat too long in the take-out box. Once the noodles absorb nearly all the broth, remove the wok from the heat. Cover the wok with a lid and let sit for 5 minutes more. The rice noodles will steam in their own residual heat and take on a chewier, springier texture.

4 Taste and adjust the seasoning as needed. Transfer to a serving plate and garnish with cilantro leaves. Serve immediately, with black vinegar and extra white pepper on the side.

Serves 6 to 8 as part of a spread

4 dried shiitake mushrooms (10g)

1¼ cups warm water

3 Tbsp neutral oil

1 scallion (20g), white and green parts separated, cut into 1-inch segments

1 (1-inch) chunk carrot (30g), julienned

¼ yellow onion (50g), sliced ¼ inch thick

⅛ head green cabbage (150g), cut into ½-inch-thick strips

¼ peeled and seeded pumpkin (150g), cut into ¼-inch-thick matchsticks

1 tsp light soy sauce

½ tsp salt

1 tsp (5g) Fried Shallots 油蔥 (page 175)

1 bundle (100g) dried thin Taiwanese rice noodles 細炊粉

⅛ tsp white pepper, plus more for serving

Cilantro leaves, for garnish

Taiwanese black vinegar 烏醋, for serving

五柳居 wǔliǔjū | ngóo-liú-ki

Five Willow Fried Fish

This dish is one that A-Má made often, and many would agree that it captures the essence of home in southern Taiwan. The focus is on the sauce, a velvety sour and faintly sweet, faintly spicy concoction, with ingredients in strips like leaves flowing off a willow tree. Tofu skin and enoki mushrooms make up the body of the "fish," and although it won't taste like fish, it has tender and juicy layers that soak up the sauce just as well as fish would. The size of your tofu sheet determines how large your fish will be, and if you can find one that is half-moon-shaped (bànyuán dòupí 半圓豆皮), you won't have to trim it. The practice of making a vegetarian fish is deeply rooted in Taiwanese prayer culture.

Serves 4 to 6 as part of a spread

Fish Filling

2 Tbsp neutral oil

5 oz (140g) fresh tofu skin rolls 豆包

3½ oz (100g) enoki mushrooms, cut into 1½- to 2-inch segments

¼ tsp salt

1 Tbsp all-purpose flour

Wrapping and Frying

3 cups plus 1 Tbsp neutral oil

2 Tbsp (15g) all-purpose flour

2 Tbsp water

1 (10- to 11-inch) square sheet dried tofu skin 千張/腐皮

1 (7- to 8-inch) square sheet nori (seaweed) 海苔

Sauce

4 dried shiitake mushrooms (10g)

3 cups warm All-Purpose Stock 高湯 (page 150) or water

1 To make the fish filling: In a wok or a nonstick pan over medium heat, warm the neutral oil until hot. Add the tofu skin rolls and fry for about 1 minute on each side, until golden and puffed. Transfer them to a plate to cool. Add the enoki mushrooms to the wok and stir-fry for 3 to 5 minutes, until they are lightly browned and fragrant and the steam dissipates. Transfer to a medium bowl.

2 Using a pair of scissors, snip the tofu skin rolls along the grain into ½-inch-wide strips. Add them to the bowl with the enoki mushrooms and mix in the salt and all-purpose flour. Set aside.

3 To make the wrapping: Brush a large plate with 1 Tbsp of the neutral oil. In a small bowl, combine the all-purpose flour and water. Mix until no lumps remain and set aside. On a dry work surface, lay the sheet of dried tofu skin flat. Trim the tofu skin to make a rough outline of a fish (see photos on page 200). Lay the nori on top of the tofu skin and check the size—you want to leave about a 1-inch border between the edge of the nori and the tofu skin. Trim the nori sheet as needed. Brush one side of the nori with the flour slurry, then quickly flip it over and stick it to

(continued)

(continued)

Five Willow Fried Fish —— continued

the very center of the tofu sheet. ❷ Brush the whole surface of the nori with a thin layer of the flour slurry and add the fish filling mixture on top of the nori. ❸ Fold the bottom half of the tofu sheet over the filling, ❹ brush the slurry on the side now on top, and ❺ roll upward to create the fish's body. ❻ For the fish head, stick the loose ends together and shape into a snoutlike structure. For the fish tail, twist where the nori ends. Once complete, make three shallow diagonal scores 1 to 1½ inches long on the body. Transfer the fish to the oiled plate. (You can prepare the fish up to this point several hours ahead of time and store covered in the refrigerator until ready to eat.)

4 To prepare the sauce: In a small bowl, soak the dried shiitake mushrooms in the warm stock for 20 to 30 minutes, until fully soft. Drain the mushrooms, reserving the stock. Snip off and discard the stems and cut the caps into thin batons. The dried mushrooms will expand significantly when cooking, so it's best to keep these very thin. Set the mushrooms and their soaking liquid aside separately. In a medium bowl, rinse the julienned potatoes with running water to rid them of excess starch. The water will quickly turn murky. Pour the murky water out, refill the bowl with fresh water, and soak for 30 minutes. Drain the potatoes and set them aside.

5 Place the fish in a bamboo steamer (or a steel steamer or on a metal steaming stand). Set the steamer over a large pot of boiling water and steam on high for 10 minutes. The purpose of steaming here is to make sure the flour has time to cook and gelatinize (if it hasn't, you will taste some grainy, uncooked bits at the end). Transfer the fish onto a paper towel–lined plate and allow the surface to dry.

6 In a wok over medium-high heat, warm the remaining 3 cups neutral oil to 320° to 338°F (160° to 170°C). Very carefully lower the fish into the hot oil and fry for 1 to 2 minutes, flipping once, until golden and crispy on all sides. Carefully lift the fish out of the hot oil using a spider strainer and place it onto an oblong fish dish to cool.

(continued)

1 small peeled russet potato (50g), julienned

1 Tbsp neutral oil

6 garlic cloves, roughly diced

¼ yellow onion (50g), thinly sliced

2 oz (60g) shelled and cooked bamboo shoots, julienned

1 oz (30g) wood ear fungus 木耳, thinly sliced

1 (1-inch) chunk carrot (30g), julienned

1 Tbsp golden granulated sugar

1 tsp light soy sauce

2 tsp potato starch 太白粉 or cornstarch

2 Tbsp water

1 fresh red chili (5g to 10g), thinly sliced on a bias

2 Tbsp Taiwanese black vinegar 烏醋, preferably Wu Yin brand, 五印醋

¼ tsp salt

¼ tsp white pepper

½ tsp sesame oil 香油

-

Handful Taiwanese basil 九層塔 or Thai basil

Five Willow Fried Fish —— continued

7 Set a wok over medium heat and heat it until it just starts smoking. Ladle in the 1 Tbsp neutral oil and swirl it around to create a nonstick surface. Add the garlic and fry for 1 to 2 minutes to brown the cloves on all sides. Add the yellow onion and fry for 1 minute, until just beginning to turn translucent. Add the bamboo shoots, wood ear fungus, carrot, and sugar and swirl in the light soy sauce, tossing everything together a few times to combine. Pour in the mushroom-soaking liquid, bring to a gentle boil, and cook for about 5 minutes to infuse all the flavors. When the time is nearly up, make a slurry with the potato starch and water. Drizzle in the slurry while constantly stirring until the sauce thickens. Mix in the red chili slices, black vinegar, salt, and white pepper to the wok and cook for 45 seconds to infuse all the flavors. Add the potatoes, mixing and stirring for about 30 seconds, until they just start to soften and bend. Taste and adjust the seasoning as needed. Remove from the heat and finish with the sesame oil.

8 Ladle the sauce over the vegetarian fried fish. Garnish with basil leaves and serve immediately. Cool any leftovers and store them in an airtight container in the refrigerator for up to 3 days.

a

b

c

d

e

Food as Supplement

Taiwan has a culture of *sit-póo* (食補)—using food to maintain health, as opposed to clinical methods. The intention is to incorporate medicinal herbs into one's everyday diet and get to the root of the illness before it strikes, rather than simply responding when a situation arises. Just as food is medicine, cooks are doctors, too. In traditional Chinese medicine (TCM), there are four main energy attributes in food: hán (cold), liáng (cool), wēn (warm), and rè (hot). When you consume from one group, its energy nature will have a corresponding effect on your body. To arrive at a healthy balance, the elderly often say, you should be mindful of these natures. Vegetables tend to veer toward hán (cold) and meat toward rè (hot). Eating a vegetable-based diet year-round can turn your body "colder," weakening your blood and energy circulation. Knowing this, many Taiwanese vegetarians and Buddhist nuns adopt a year-round habit of imbibing *póo-thng* (補湯), herbal soups that are warming in nature. Some people have the impression that TCM herbs are no different from eating medicine, but that is far from the truth. Many TCM herbs are not only healthful totems but also culinary powerhouses, each with their own distinctive flavors and textures. Used appropriately, they enrich cooking just as any spice would. You can find all the TCM herbs you need for the recipes in this book online or, better yet, at local Asian retail markets. Show the formula to the staff and they will help you assemble what you need.

Note: TCM herbs are not for everyone. Treat them as supplements rather than cures for serious illness. People who are immunocompromised should either consult an expert before using the herbs or avoid them altogether.

麻辣火鍋 málà huǒguō
Mala Hot Pot

The flavor profile of málà hot pot comes from the tingly spike (má) of Sichuan peppercorns and heat (là) from the piles of dried chilies, though this one won't make you lose any nerve endings in your lips. The TCM herbs here are meant not only to bolster health but also to soothe the stomach from all the chilies' heat. This málà broth, as is typical with many Taiwanese-style versions, is somewhat sweet. Both the málà broth and the milder broth get better as you cook more ingredients and layer the flavors; I love combining them in my bowl and drinking it like a soup.

Note: The quality of Sichuan peppercorns can vary a lot. You'll know it's high quality when their citrusy aroma comes flooding your nostrils as soon as you put your nose near. There is also a distinction between red and green Sichuan peppercorns: red is more fragrant than tingly, and green is more tingly than fragrant; you can mix them and play with proportions to your preference. If you add the full amount called for in the recipe and still find the flavor and/or tingle to be insufficient, you can add more peppercorns directly into the broth as it is cooking.

1 You can hot pot with any wide pot, but it's nice to have a divided pot in which you can serve two separate broths, for everyone to encircle. You'll need a couple of mesh skimmer spoons, long chopsticks, soup ladles, plus a portable stove for cooking at the table; both electrical and gas stoves will work, though we tend to use the latter for extra ambiance points.

2 Start the day before. Make the All-Purpose Stock (page 150). Also make any add-ons you'd like that need to be prepared ahead of time; look through the Vegetarian Meat section (page 54).

3 To make the mild broth: In a large pot, combine the stock, daikon radish, corn, gan cao, and hong zao. Bring to a boil over high heat, lower

(continued)

Serves 4 to 6

Mild Broth

6¼ cups All-Purpose Stock 高湯 (page 150)

1 medium peeled daikon radish (400g), quartered lengthwise and cut into 1-inch chunks

1 large ear corn (200g), husked and cut into 2-inch chunks

4 pieces gan cao (dried licorice root)

5 hong zao (dried red dates)

1 tsp salt, or to taste

2 tsp goji berries

2 scallions, green parts only, cut into 1-inch segments

Mala Broth

6¼ cups All-Purpose Stock 高湯 (page 150)

1 cup (200g) Mala Base 麻辣鍋底 (recipe follows) or use store-bought (prepare according to the package directions)

(continued)

Mala Hot Pot —— continued

the heat to medium-low or low, and simmer for 35 to 45 minutes, until the daikon is tender and slightly translucent. Season with salt. Pour into one side of the divided hot pot. Add the goji berries and green scallion segments before serving.

4 To make the mala broth: In a large pot, combine the stock and mala base. Bring to a boil over high heat, lower the heat to medium-low or low, and simmer for 40 minutes to infuse all the flavors. Strain through a fine-mesh sieve into the other side of the divided hot pot. If you find the broth is too spicy or pungent, add a pinch of MSG to balance the flavor. Add the scallion whites before serving.

Pinch of MSG (as needed)

2 scallions, white parts only, sliced on a bias

-

Ingredients of choice (see page 207), for serving

Preparing Ingredients and Sauces

While the broths are simmering, prepare the spread of ingredients you'll serve alongside the broth. I like to have lots of tofu and tofu-related products, like frozen tofu (medium-firm tofu cut into 1-inch cubes and frozen overnight), fresh or fried tofu skin rolls or dòugān (bean curd), and an array of store-bought vegetarian meatballs; vegetables such as green cabbage, romaine lettuce, chrysanthemum (Tong Ho), or napa cabbage (all cut into roughly 2-inch pieces) or broccoli or cauliflower (torn into bite-size florets). I also like to have ears of corn (cut into 2-inch segments), fresh tomatoes, and a mix of mushrooms (shiitake, king oyster, shimeji, enoki, etc.)—these lend umami and sweet flavors to the broth. Serve a bowl of hot steamed rice for each person, or if your crowd prefers noodles, serve udon, ramen, konjak, or cellophane noodles on platters. Dad always likes to add a packet of instant noodles at the end of the meal, for anyone not yet full or satisfied.

Prepare separate bowls of chopped fresh aromatics and condiments of your choice. I like to make two dipping sauces: one with light soy sauce as a base, a small splash of black vinegar, generous pinches of chopped scallions, minced ginger, minced garlic, and a spoonful of chili oil (page 95), especially if we're not eating the Mala Hot Pot on page 205; the other with equal parts light soy sauce and vegetarian sha-cha sauce, a drizzle of sesame oil, plus a sprinkle of chopped fresh cilantro and peanut sugar (see page 104).

When ready to serve, pour the broths into the pot and set it on the table over the portable stove. Bring to a rolling boil and add the first set of ingredients—those that take longer to cook, basically anything that isn't leafy green vegetables, which can just be added when desired. Keep the broth simmering as you cook and eat.

麻辣鍋底 málà guōdǐ

Mala Base

1 Put on a pair of gloves and a face mask. Touching the chilies with your bare hands or inhaling their fumes can cause awful irritations.

2 In a medium bowl, combine the green Sichuan peppercorns, gan cao, dong quai, chuanxiong, and your additional spices of choice. Rinse with cool water to get rid of any dust and then drain. Set aside.

3 To prepare the dried chilies, pick out and discard any discolored or moldy-looking ones. In a medium bowl, soak the dried èrjīngtiáo chilies in enough warm water to cover for 20 minutes, until softened. Drain, discard the soaking water, and transfer the chilies to a blender. Pulse a few times to chop the chilies into small flakes. Set aside.

4 In a wok over medium to medium-low heat, warm the neutral oil and the sesame oil. Add the ginger and red chilies and fry for 1 to 2 minutes to release their fragrance. Add the chopped dried red chilies and dòubànjiàng and fry together at a slow bubble for 10 minutes, by which point the oil should be stained a dark red. Add the fermented black soybeans and peanut butter and cook for 5 minutes at a slow bubble to infuse all the flavors. Add the rock sugar and rice cooking wine and cook, still at a slow bubble, for 1 to 2 minutes. Add all the herbs and spices, stirring to combine, and cook for 5 minutes more, until very fragrant. Remove from the heat and set aside to cool.

5 Once slightly cooled, transfer the mixture to the blender. Blend for 15 to 30 seconds, until you get a homogenous paste. Don't blend it too finely—you should still be able to see flecks of the herbs and some whole peppercorns.

6 Ladle the finished mala base into a lidded airtight 4-cup glass container. Refrigerate for at least 2 days before using to allow flavors to infuse. Store for up to 2 months in the refrigerator or for up to 6 months in the freezer.

Makes about 4 cups (1,000g)

⅓ cup (20g) green Sichuan peppercorns

6 pieces gan cao (dried licorice root) (6g)

1 small piece dong quai (female ginseng) (4g)

2 whole chuanxiong (Sichuan lovage) (4g)

one recipe Five-Spice or Thirteen-Spice (page 27)

2 cups (40g) dried red èrjīngtiáo chilies 二荊條

1 cup neutral oil

¼ cup sesame oil 香油

2 (1-inch) pieces peeled ginger (40g), sliced

4 red chilies (40g), chopped

1 cup (240g) dòubànjiàng (chili bean paste) 豆瓣醬

1 Tbsp (10g) fermented black soybeans 蔭豉/豆豉

2 Tbsp (35g) peanut butter

¼ cup (50g) rock sugar

¼ cup Taiwanese rice cooking wine, preferably 19.5 percent ABV

薑母鍋 jiāngmǔguō | kiunn-bú-ko

Herbal Ginger Hot Pot

When it's winter in Taiwan, you imbibe an herbal hot pot. Ginger, sesame oil, and rice cooking wine are the holy trinity of Taiwanese medicinal cooking, and it's a powerful combination that will offset any sense of coldness in your body or limbs. The broth is always served steaming hot, yet somehow refreshing and gently sweet. Sitting huddled around the bubbling cauldron seems to warm up the soul, too. When you drink the broth, there's a restorative power that flushes through your sinuses and a cinnamon-ginseng warmth that makes you feel as if you're getting stronger and healthier with each sip.

Notes: Tradition calls for old ginger that has been delayed harvest (it stays in the ground between 1 and 3 years and, hence, is called the "mother"). You don't necessarily need to source a ginger mother, but know that the older, the better: it has stronger medicinal properties and a more intense flavor. For an extra kick, blend up some ginger and strain it into the broth at the very end. Rice cooking wine amounts will have to be lowered if yours is salted. Add shàngtāng (Superior Stock, page 151) to compensate.

1 Don't peel the ginger—most of the ginger's flavor and medicinal properties come from right underneath its skin. Instead, brush the skins clean with a vegetable brush or an unused toothbrush. On a cutting board, lay each piece flat and, using a heavy rolling pin or the flat side of a cleaver, smack them one by one until all the ginger is crumbled into pieces no larger than ¼ inch.

2 To prepare the herbs and spices: Place the cinnamon stick, cinnamon twigs, and fennel seeds into a braising pouch or on a small piece of cheesecloth. Tie a knot to secure it and set aside. Combine the remaining herbs and spices on a plate and set it aside as well.

(continued)

Serves 6 to 8 as a hot pot

10½ oz (300g) old ginger

Herbs and Spices

2 (1-inch) pieces cinnamon stick (4g)

4½ Tbsp (18g) gui zhi (cinnamon twigs)

2 tsp (5g) fennel seeds

6 whole pieces chuanxiong (Sichuan lovage) (11g)

½ piece dong quai (female ginseng) (4g)

6 ren shen xu (ginseng roots) (5g)

28 slices huang qi (astragalus root) (19g)

6 sticks dangshen (codonopsis root) (11g)

1 piece shu di huang (rehmannia root) (5g)

12 pieces gan cao (dried licorice root) (11g)

2 Tbsp (16g) shan nai (sand ginger)

-

½ cup toasted black sesame oil 黑麻油

(continued)

209
Mains

Herbal Ginger Hot Pot —— continued

3 In a large pot over medium heat, warm the toasted sesame oil. Add the ginger and fry slowly, just gently bubbling, for about 15 minutes, until very fragrant, mostly dry, and reduced to about half of their original size. Add the braising pouch, the remaining herbs and spices, and fry for 5 minutes more. Add the rice cooking wine, adjust the heat to high, and bring to a boil. Add the black dates. Adjust the heat to medium or medium-low and cook, uncovered, at a gentle boil for 30 minutes.

4 Meanwhile, to prepare the dipping sauce: In a blender, blend the fermented bean curd, dòubànjiàng, water, and granulated sugar until smooth. Set aside.

5 Return to your broth and, using a slotted spoon, fish out the loose fragments of ginger skin floating at the surface. Take out about half of the loose herbs and spices as well, to give space for the other ingredients. Add the stock, salt, and MSG (if using) and stir well to combine. Add the frozen tofu, lion's mane mushrooms, and corn and cook for 30 minutes.

6 Add the gluten threads, enoki mushrooms, and green cabbage to the pot and cook for 3 to 5 minutes, until the green cabbage is just soft but still has a crunchy bite. Taste the broth and dilute it with some water if it is too rich or too alcoholic for your taste. Add the goji berries. Serve over a hot pot stove, with the dipping sauce and sesame oil vermicelli (recipe follows) on the side, plus other ingredients of your choice for cooking at the table.

5 cups Taiwanese rice cooking wine, preferably 19.5 percent ABV

8 oblong black dates (40g)

5 cups Superior Stock 上湯 (page 151)

1½ tsp salt

Pinch of MSG (optional)

1 (400g) block frozen tofu

7 oz (200g) Lion's Mane Mushrooms 猴頭菇 (page 62)

1 large ear corn (180g), husked and cut into 2-inch segments

3½ oz (100g) Gluten Threads 皮絲 (page 59)

7 oz (200g) enoki mushrooms

¼ head green cabbage (300g)

1½ Tbsp (15g) goji berries

Dipping Sauce

8 cubes spicy fermented bean curd in sesame oil 麻油辣腐乳 (120g)

2 tsp dòubànjiàng (chili bean paste) 豆瓣醬

2 tsp water

4 tsp golden granulated sugar

(continued)

(continued)

麻油麵線 máyóu miànxiàn ┃ muâ-iû-mī-suànn

Sesame Oil Vermicelli

Miànxiàn, sometimes called "long-life noodles," are salt-bolstered wheat noodles stretched into long, chewy strands as thin as hair. A heaped plate is always served next to a ginger hot pot. They're very salty, so make sure you boil them with lots of water!

Serves 3 or 4 as part of a spread

1 Rinse the noodles two or three times to get rid of excess salt. Drain and set aside.

2 In a small saucepan over medium-low heat, warm the toasted sesame oil. Add the sliced ginger and sizzle slowly for 5 to 7 minutes, until fragrant and curled. Remove the saucepan from the heat and mix in the fried shallots. Set aside.

3 Bring a large pot of water to a rolling boil over high heat. Add the vermicelli and cook in the rapidly boiling water for 30 to 60 seconds, to your desired doneness. Using tongs or chopsticks, transfer the vermicelli straight into the warm ginger hot pot broth and soak for 1 minute.

4 Transfer the noodles into the saucepan with the sesame oil, ginger, and shallots. Toss everything together and, using a pair of scissors, snip the noodles once roughly at the center of the bundle to cut them in half. Transfer to a serving plate. Garnish with chopped scallions and/or cilantro leaves and serve immediately.

1 bundle (about 75g) Taiwanese long-life noodles 麵線

1 Tbsp toasted sesame oil, preferably toasted black sesame oil 黑麻油

1 (1-inch) piece unpeeled ginger (10g), thinly sliced

1 tsp (5g) Fried Shallots 油蔥 (page 175)

Ginger hot pot broth (see page 209), kept warm

Chopped scallions, green parts only, and/or cilantro leaves, for garnish

Festival and Food

A-Gong need not say it. We all knew the round table was the centerpiece of our Tamsui home. The surface of the table is the cross-section of a rosewood branch that A-Gong carried on a truck across the island, all the way from Kaohsiung to Taipei. It has a glass turntable on top that works smooth as clockwork and tattoos on each leg with patterns of flower and vine. He built the table with celebration in mind. Only six people lived in the house, and the table has seats for more than fifteen. It was so large that it felt out of place; you couldn't easily walk to the other end of the room when all the chairs were pulled out. But on the few days of the year that we celebrated our traditional festivals, all the seats were filled and there wasn't an inch to spare in the room. He wanted everyone to come home and eat.

Spring Festival

Tshun-tseh (春節) or Spring Festival is Taiwan's largest traditional holiday. Its history traces back to agrarian times, when it signaled the beginning of spring, the end of a year's worth of farmwork, and the end of the lunar calendar. As kids, we were regaled with stories of a horrendous lionlike monster called Niánshòu (年獸) that came out from the mountains on the last night of the lunar calendar to eat people. I used to be so afraid of the beast that I couldn't sleep. The beast hated the color red and loud, banging sounds, so to scare it away on the last night of the year, I duly helped decorate our house with

215

red paper and stayed up until midnight to set off firecrackers.

While the legend is probably not real (and certainly a terrible bedtime story), the New Year remained a special time for our family. It was a time filled with superstitions and traditions. On the day of New Year's Eve (除夕), every family was busy at work. We vacuumed the entire house and wiped every corner until it was shining. If your house was clean for the first few days of the New Year, fortune would pile in, and you wouldn't want to sweep any of that luck out. Even the garbage cans wouldn't be emptied for a few days.

For my family, the most important tradition of New Year's Eve was the food and prayers. Before sundown, my mom would prepare a table's worth of food offerings to show gratitude to Guanyin (a bodhisattva) and our ancestors. We lit up incense sticks and prayed for their blessings. I remember this clearly as we—the *sun-á* (孫仔, grandkids)—were responsible for asking the gods and spirits whether they were happy with their meal. There were two crescent-moon-shaped blocks (*puáh-pue* 筊杯) that we threw on the floor as communication tokens. The blocks each had one curved side and one flat side, and their orientations indicated the response. One curved side and one flat side up meant "yes," two curved sides up meant "no," and two flat sides up meant "laughing." My brother had the most blessed hands. He usually got a "yes" on the first try.

We used to pray with all kinds of meat—whole cuts of chicken, pork, and fish were traditional—but after A-Gong passed, we switched to vegetarian dishes. A bubbling hot pot was still the centerpiece, which symbolized tuányuán (團圓, reunion and togetherness). A whole vegetarian fish (see Five Willow Fried Fish, page 197) carried the pomp and meaning of surplus (年年有餘), the same way a whole steamed fish does. Oranges symbolized prosperity (大吉大利), so we ate them daily. In place of buying whole cuts of mock chicken or pork, which our family didn't prefer, my mom assigned her own meanings to different fruits and vegetables. We ate eggplants, as old Taiwanese proverbs referred to them as instilling vigor and positive energy (吃茄會揪抖). We also ate string beans, because the round seeds inside the pod were neatly arranged like cute little babies, and they reminded my mom of a full family. We abided by old traditions and made some of our own in this new vegetarian setting.

油飯 yóufàn | iû-pn̄g

Taiwanese Sticky Rice

The only time A-Gong resisted the urge to eat *han-tsî-bê* (Sweet Potato Congee, page 67) was the New Year. During this period, everything is symbolic, and congee represented poverty and less fortunate times. Yóufàn, a symbol of celebration, takes the stage as the main dish instead. Chewy, fragrant grains of sticky rice are imbued with a mild nutty sweetness from the chestnuts and cashews. I love that it's the centerpiece of a New Year's spread and, at the same time, humble and comforting enough for any ordinary day.

1 In a medium bowl, rinse the sticky rice three to five times, or until the water runs mostly clear. Drain, add the cashews, and soak in water to cover by at least 2 inches for 4 hours or up to overnight.

2 Soak the dried shiitake mushrooms in the warm water for 20 to 30 minutes, until fully soft. Drain the mushrooms, reserving the water. Snip off and discard the stems and thinly slice the caps. Set the mushrooms and their soaking liquid aside separately.

3 Set a wok over medium heat and heat it until it just starts smoking. Swirl in both the neutral oil and the toasted sesame oil. Add the shiitake mushrooms and stir-fry for 3 to 5 minutes to release their fragrance. Swirl in the light soy sauce and cook for 1 minute, until the fragrance has deepened. Swirl in the rice cooking wine as well and boil for 1 to 2 minutes to cook off the alcohol. Add the mushroom-soaking liquid to the wok. Bring to a boil and cook for 5 to 7 minutes, until the liquid reduces by about half and darkens in color. Set aside.

4 Strain the sticky rice and cashews and spread them out in a cloth-lined bamboo steamer. Use your fingertips to make holes throughout, to allow better heat circulation (the holes should be deep enough so that you can see the bottom cloth). Spread the chestnuts on top of the rice. Cover the rice with the hanging edges of the cloth, then secure the lid. Set the

Serves 6 to 8 as part of a spread

1⅓ cups (300g) long-grain sticky/glutinous rice 長糯米

¼ cup (38g) raw cashews

8 dried shiitake mushrooms (20g)

1 cup warm water

2 Tbsp neutral oil

1 Tbsp toasted sesame oil 麻油, preferably toasted black sesame oil 黑麻油

2 Tbsp light soy sauce

⅓ cup Taiwanese rice cooking wine, preferably 19.5 percent ABV

6 fresh shelled chestnuts 栗子 (60g), halved, or 12 dried, soaked overnight and kept whole

2 Tbsp (30g) Fried Shallots 油蔥 (page 175) or use store-bought

Chopped cilantro, for serving

Sweet Chili Sauce 甜辣醬 (page 17), for serving

(continued)

Taiwanese Sticky Rice —— continued

steamer over boiling water on high heat and steam for 25 to 30 minutes, until the rice grains are translucent and tender.

5 Return the wok with the sauce to medium heat. Bring to a boil and add the steamed sticky rice mixture. Lower the heat to low or medium-low and, using chopsticks, stir to incorporate, being careful not to mash the now-tender grains. Once all the sauce is absorbed and evenly distributed, mix in the fried shallots. Scoop the sticky rice back onto the cloth in the bamboo steamer and steam for 5 to 10 minutes over boiling water on high heat to infuse all the flavors, or until the grains are at your desired softness.

6 Serve in the steamer, with chopped cilantro on top and sweet chili sauce on the side for drizzling and eating. Cool any leftovers and store them in an airtight container in the refrigerator for up to 5 days.

佛跳牆 fótiàoqiáng

Buddha Jump over the Wall

This dish, originally from Fuzhou in China's Fujian Province, is so named because it is such an incredible combination of precious meat, poultry, and seafood that a Buddhist monk would jump over the wall upon smelling it. This vegetarian version would equally tempt the monk, but he wouldn't need to slip over the wall to sample it. It's packed with umami from a simple mix of vegetables, mushrooms, seeds, and nuts. Dong quai supplies fragrance and brings a healthful warmness, just as a chicken broth would in the original non-vegetarian recipe. Serving it in a tureen (甕) completes the dish. See the photograph on page 214.

1 In a medium bowl, soak the dried shiitake mushrooms in the warm water for 20 to 30 minutes, until fully soft. Drain the mushrooms, reserving the water. Snip off and discard the stems. Set the mushrooms and their soaking water aside separately.

2 In a medium bowl, rinse the preserved bamboo shoots three or four times, until the water turns from a murky yellow to a faint off-white. Soak the shoots in water for 15 to 20 minutes. Drain the bamboo shoots and set them aside.

3 Prepare a medium bowl with 2 cups water and the rice vinegar. Using the back of a knife, scrape off the brown exterior skin of the burdock root, taking care to keep the off-white interior skin intact. Cut on a diagonal into ¼-inch-thick slices and add each piece to the prepared bowl of diluted vinegar as you cut to prevent oxidation. Drain the burdock slices once you're finished with cutting, move them into a bowl of fresh water, and set aside to soak until ready to use.

4 Bring a medium pot with 4 cups water to a rolling boil. Blanch the napa cabbage for 15 to 20 seconds, until just wilted. Using a spider strainer or slotted spoon, transfer the cabbage to a plate and set aside. Add the

(continued)

Serves 6 to 8 as part of a spread

8 dried shiitake mushrooms (20g)

5 cups warm water

2 oz (60g) preserved bamboo shoot ends 筍茸, preferably from ma bamboo shoots 麻竹筍

1 Tbsp rice vinegar

3½ oz (100g) burdock root 牛蒡

¼ small head napa cabbage (150g), cut into 2-inch pieces

1 Tbsp neutral oil

6 (1-inch) slices peeled ginger (10g)

3½ oz (100g) shimeji mushrooms

2 tsp light soy sauce

1½ tsp salt

3½ oz (100g) baby corn, husked and kept whole

5 oz (150g) fried tofu

1 small piece dong quai (female ginseng) (3g)

⅓ cup (50g) raw cashews

(continued)

preserved bamboo shoots to the pot and boil for 15 minutes. Drain, rinse, and set aside.

5 In the same pot over medium heat, warm the neutral oil. Add the ginger and stir-fry for about 30 seconds, until fragrant. Add the shimeji mushrooms and fry for 2 to 4 minutes to release their fragrance. Strain the shiitake-soaking liquid through a fine-mesh sieve and into the pot. Add the soy sauce and salt and bring to a boil. Taste and adjust the seasonings as needed.

6 Meanwhile, nestle the following ingredients into a tureen or large bowl in this order: napa cabbage, bamboo shoots, burdock, baby corn, fried tofu, dong quai, cashews, chestnuts, and lotus seeds. Using a slotted spoon, remove the shimeji mushrooms and ginger from the broth and add those to the tureen. Follow with the cordyceps flower, bamboo fungus, lion's mane mushrooms, shiitake mushrooms, hong zao, and gingko.

7 Once the broth comes to a boil, pour it into the tureen. Cover the top with a plate. Steam in a large rice cooker or steel steamer for 40 minutes. Serve hot in the tureen. Cool any leftovers and store in an airtight container in the refrigerator for up to 3 days.

10 fresh shelled chestnuts (100g), or use dried that are soaked overnight

20 fresh or dried lotus seeds (20g)

¼ cup (5g) dried cordyceps flower 黃金蟲草花

2 dried bamboo fungus 竹笙 (5g), ends trimmed, cut into 4 pieces

3½ oz (100g) Lion's Mane Mushrooms 猴頭菇 (page 62)

4 hong zao (dried red dates) (15g)

10 fresh gingko nuts (20g), or use dried that have been soaked overnight

長年菜湯 chángniáncài tāng | tn̂g-nî-tshài-thng

Long-Life Mustard Greens Soup

Serves 8 to 10

The first time I tried this soup, I hated it. A-Gong spooned it toward my mouth at a New Year's Eve dinner and said, "You must have a sip for long life!" It was bitter and acrid and what I imagined a stagnant pond tasted like. Each day, A-Gong added new mustard leaves and sometimes sweet potato or kabocha squash chunks to the broth. He cooked it over and over, until the old greens were so tender that they melted between my teeth. Their umami sweetness slowly subsumed the bitterness, and I started to grasp the essence of the dish. As the proverb *khóo-tsīn kam-lâi* (苦盡甘來) goes: When the hardship is over, good things will come. See the photograph on page 214.

4 dried shiitake mushrooms (10g)

5 cups warm All-Purpose Stock 高湯 (page 150)

1 head swatow mustard 大芥菜/刈菜 (650g), stems and leaves separated, cut on a bias into 2 to 3-inch pieces

2 Tbsp neutral oil

1 (1-inch) piece peeled ginger (20g), sliced

2 Tbsp Taiwanese rice cooking wine

1½ tsp salt, plus more as needed

Pinch of MSG (optional)

1 In a small bowl, soak the dried shiitake mushrooms in the warm stock for 20 to 30 minutes, until fully soft. Drain the mushrooms, reserving the stock. Snip off the stems and set aside the mushrooms and the stock separately.

2 Bring a tall pot with 4 cups water to a boil. Blanch the mustard stems for about 30 seconds, just until they turn bright green. Drain and rinse with cold water. Set aside.

3 In the same pot over medium-high heat, warm the neutral oil. Add the ginger slices and fry for 15 to 30 seconds, until fragrant. Add the mustard stems, mustard leaves, mushrooms, and the mushroom-soaking liquid and bring to a rolling boil. Adjust the heat to a slow boil, add the rice cooking wine and season with salt and MSG (if using). Cook uncovered for 20 to 25 minutes, until the greens are thoroughly wilted. Taste and adjust the seasonings as needed. Transfer to a bowl or clay pot and serve immediately. Cool any leftovers and store in an airtight container in the refrigerator for up to 3 days.

On Rice and Rice Cakes (kué 粿)

It is no secret that a great rice cake requires whole grains of rice. You can smell the rice's fragrance and feel its chew in a finished product, whereas if you used pre-ground rice flour, you get something that tastes flat and often slightly moldy. This isn't simply because the rice flour is factory processed; it is because you have no way of knowing the quality and source of the rice.

You'll find short-grain japonica rice (gēngmǐ 粳米), like Penglai rice (Pénglaimǐ 蓬萊米), which has a pleasing texture when steamed, on our dinner table nightly, but we tend to use different ones for our rice cakes. We'll often use a long-grain indica rice (xiānmǐ 秈米) that is fluffy and loose, similar to basmati rice. Chailai rice (zàiláimǐ 在來米), meaning "the original rice," is the local cultivar we use. Because of its high amylose content, chailai rice cooks up to a rather tough bite, making it not so nice to eat on its own and thus the rice of choice for producing rice cakes. To achieve the perfect "Q" (springy) texture for rice cakes, the grains are aged in their husks for more than a year, until they dehydrate and harden, in addition to taking on some complex chemical changes. This isn't the same as letting your bag of rice sit in the larder for a while; doing so will just turn its oils rancid. Glutinous rice (nuòmǐ 糯米), which also appears in many rice cake recipes, differs by variety in the same way. Short-grain glutinous rice (gēngnuò 粳糯 or yuánnuò 圓糯) is softer and stickier than long-grain glutinous rice (xiānnuò 秈糯 or chángnuò 長糯). You can, of course, still use rice or glutinous rice flours. Use water milled for its finer ground. Take the weight from the weight of the rice called for in recipes, and mix it with the water to make the slurry or dough.

年糕 niángāo | 甜米果 tinn-kué
New Year Rice Cake

Steaming the New Year rice cake is a time-consuming and sacred task, so there are lots of traditions surrounding it. For example, you're not supposed to say negative words while the rice cake is steaming, or you can anger the deity living in the kitchen stove and cause the cake to fail. I have a lot of good memories of this sweet rice cake from childhood, perhaps because we would eat this around the same time that the hóngbāo (紅包, red envelopes filled with money) were distributed. Mom sliced up the rice cake and deep-fried it into puffy, crunchy golden nuggets. I took bite after bite, seeing how long I could pull the sugar strings. It's warm, gooey, and sweet, and it made New Year's Eve infinitely more special. Plan to make this 2 to 3 days in advance—it needs time to harden before you can cut into it.

Makes one 6-inch cake

1¼ cup (300g) short-grain (round) sticky/glutinous rice 圓糯米

1¼ cups water

¾ cup (150g) golden granulated sugar

⅓ cup (65g) dark brown sugar 黑糖, blended until fine if clumped

1 cup (120g) cake flour, plus more for dusting

6 Tbsp (60g) glutinous rice flour 糯米粉

1 tsp (4g) baking powder

14 Tbsp cold water

3 cups plus 2 tsp neutral oil

1 In a medium bowl, rinse the sticky rice three to five times, until the water runs mostly clear. Drain and soak the rice in the 1¼ cups of water for at least 6 hours and up to overnight. If it is hot outside, refrigerate while soaking—you want the rice to be cold so the blending won't cause it to cook prematurely.

2 In a blender, blend the rice and its soaking liquid on high for 2 to 4 minutes, until you get a thick, smooth rice slurry. Pour the slurry through a cheesecloth and squeeze the cloth over the sink to expel all the liquid, until you get a pulp that feels like crumbled dry chalk.

3 Transfer the pulp to a large bowl. Using your hands, knead in the golden and dark brown sugars until they dissolve and the mixture takes on a dough consistency (that sort of "melts" when you pick it up) and a homogeneous brown color, 5 to 8 minutes. Line a 6-inch bamboo steamer with parchment paper.

4 Transfer the dough to the parchment-lined bamboo steamer. Drop the steamer on the counter a few times to get rid of any air bubbles. Set

(continued)

the steamer over a large pot of boiling water (make sure there is plenty of water) and steam steadily on medium heat for 2 to 2½ hours, until slightly translucent and shiny.

5   Fresh out of the steamer, the rice cake will be too soft and gooey. Let cool and refrigerate for at least 2 nights, before slicing. If you wish to eat the rice cake right away, you can twirl a pair of chopsticks into it and eat it like a lollipop!

6   To fry, cut the cake into ½-inch-thick slices, then into bite-size pieces (about 2 inches long). In a medium bowl, make the frying batter by sifting together the cake flour, rice flour, and baking powder. Add the cold water and 2 tsp of the neutral oil. Mix until a batter just forms, taking care not to overmix (and subsequently develop gluten). Set aside. In a separate small bowl, add some additional cake flour. You'll use this to dust the pieces before frying.

7   In a wok over medium-high heat, warm 3 cups of the neutral oil to 320°F (160°C), then turn down the heat to medium-low. Dust each rice cake piece with a light coating of cake flour, shake off the excess, and, using a fork, roll each piece in the frying batter and add it one by one to the hot oil to fry, making sure not to overcrowd the wok. Fry slowly for 3 to 5 minutes, flipping once, until the outer shell is lightly golden and puffed and the interior is gooey and soft.

8   Using a spider strainer or slotted spoon, lift the pieces up. Hold them over the oil as you heat the oil back to 320°F (160°C), then quickly fry the pieces once more for 10 to 15 seconds, until crisp and a prominent golden. Quickly transfer them to a wire rack to drain before the sugar starts to ooze out. Serve hot.

蘿蔔糕 luóbogāo | 菜頭粿 tshài-thâu-kué

Turnip Cake

Many New Year's symbols come from word plays. I'm compelled to think they're designed for kids to remember. When Mom passed around the turnip cakes, she'd repeat, "*Tsiáh tshài-thâu, hó-tshái-thâu* (eat daikon radishes, brings good fortune)!" The word for daikon radish (菜頭) sounds a lot like that for "harbinger of good fortune" (彩頭) in Taiwanese. I would gobble down several pieces, thinking there was possibly a multiplier effect. I like to keep my turnip cakes simple to pronounce the full flavors of the rice and daikon. To change things up, you can introduce additional tastes and fragrances, such as adding fried enoki mushrooms (see Napa Cabbage Stew, page 191) or a scoop of yóucōng (Fried Shallots, page 175). See the photograph on page 215.

Note: This dish indeed uses daikon radishes—even though the name is turnip cake. It's one of those things lost in translation. I chose to call it turnip cake here as dim sum menus use it, and my family has always called it that.

Serves 8 to 10

1¼ cups (300g) aged Taiwanese chailai indica rice 在來米 or aged basmati rice

1 cup water

1 large daikon radish (900g)

1½ tsp salt

2 Tbsp neutral oil, plus more for oiling cutting board and cake top

Sweet Chili Sauce (page 17) or Garlic Soy Paste (page 101), for serving

1 In a medium bowl, rinse the rice three to five times, until the water runs mostly clear. Drain and soak the rice in the 1 cup of water for 3 to 4 hours, until the grains are translucent throughout and easily split when pinched.

2 Peel two layers off the exterior of the daikon radish. When fully peeled, the daikon should look slightly transparent and not completely white. Don't skimp here—it's better to peel off more daikon than end up with a bitter turnip cake. Shred the daikon or cut it into very thin batons.

3 In a pot set over medium-low heat, mix the daikon and salt together. Fry gently (there should be no browning), tossing and stirring; the daikon should quickly release some liquid, allowing it to stew. Cook the daikon

gently for 8 to 10 minutes, until its liquid pools and gently bubbles in the pot, the daikon is tender and translucent, and its fragrance fills the room.

4 Meanwhile, in a blender, blend the rice and its soaking liquid on high for about 3 minutes, until you get a smooth rice slurry. When you put your hand in it, the slurry should feel only very slightly grainy or not grainy at all. Line a 7-inch bamboo steamer with parchment paper.

5 Turn off the heat and add the rice slurry to the pot. Work the mixture in the pot's residual heat, for 1 to 2 minutes, until it just thickens into a paste. Using a rubber spatula, scoop the paste into the parchment-lined bamboo steamer. Drop the steamer on the counter a few times to get rid of any air bubbles. Smooth the top and cover it with another piece of parchment (this both prevents excess condensed vapor from dripping onto the cake and keeps it moist during the steaming process). Set the steamer over a pot of boiling water and steam for 1 to 1½ hours over medium-high heat, or until a toothpick comes out mostly clean.

6 Let the turnip cake cool slightly in the bamboo steamer before transferring it to a lightly oiled cutting board. Lightly oil the top to prevent drying and cool for at least 2 hours, preferably covered overnight in the refrigerator, before slicing.

7 Slice the turnip cake into ½-inch-thick pieces, then into 2-inch-long portions. In a nonstick pan over medium heat, warm the 2 tablespoons of neutral oil. Fry the turnip cakes for 6 to 8 minutes total, until golden brown on both sides. Serve immediately with sweet chili sauce or garlic soy paste on the side for dipping. The remaining turnip cake can be stored in a lidded airtight container in the refrigerator for up to 3 days or frozen for up to 1 month.

芋丸 yùwán | ōo-uân

Fried Taro Balls

There's never enough round and spherical food on the New Year's table to signify tuányuán (團圓), reunion and togetherness. This recipe is inspired by visits we made with A-Gong to Taiwanese restaurants, where they served this at the end of the meal. I like that the roundness brings a sense of completion (yuánmǎn 圓滿). You can keep them plain, as I have here, or fill them with a sweet or savory surprise, such as dòushā (Sweet Red Bean Paste, page 245) or curry radishes (see Popiah Rolls, page 238).

1 Add the taro chunks to a bowl. Place the bowl in a bamboo steamer (or a steel steamer) and set the steamer over a large pot of boiling water. Steam the taro on high for 30 to 40 minutes, until easily pierced with a chopstick.

2 Pour out the excess water gathered in the bowl and, using a fork, quickly mash it into a paste that's mostly smooth with just a few lumps. While still hot, mix in the sugar and 5 Tbsp of the neutral oil until fully incorporated and the sugar has melted. Add the potato starch and knead by hand in the bowl for 1 minute to incorporate the starch. Divide the mixture into twenty equal portions (about 44g each) and roll them into smooth balls.

3 Line a plate with paper towels. In a wok over medium-high heat, warm the remaining 2 cups neutral oil to 355°F (180°C). Add the taro balls in batches of seven to ten and fry for 3 to 4 minutes, until golden. Using a spider strainer or slotted spoon, transfer the taro balls to the towel-lined plate to drain briefly. Serve while hot.

Makes 20 taro balls

1 (600g) peeled taro root, cut into 1- to 1½-inch chunks

½ cup (120g) golden granulated sugar

2 cups plus 5 Tbsp (75g) neutral oil, plus more as needed

7½ Tbsp (75g) potato starch 太白粉

潤餅 rùnbǐng | jūn-piánn

Popiah Rolls

This dish, eaten on Tomb-Sweeping Day (Qīngmíngjié 清明節), is to me more than just a special-occasion food; it shows how we use food to bring together our families and communities. Rùnbǐng looks like one dish, but it's an amalgamation of multiple ones. As such, it's best made with a group of people who can all take charge of their own component. I like to serve this as a spread, rather than prewrapped, so everyone can make theirs the way they like it.

Note: To cook the popiah skins, look for a cast-iron griddle that either has no or low sides. A sideless pan is traditional and ideal—it allows you to swipe your palm across the surface of the pan without catching your wrist on the hot sides. You can also use a nonstick pan, but try to find one that is older and a little winded. If the surface is too slick, the dough cannot latch on in an instant. If the wrappers look as if they're starting to dry out, steam them over high heat for 30 to 60 seconds (especially if they're one day old).

1 To make the popiah wrappers: In a large bowl, combine the bread flour, sweet potato starch, wheat germ powder, and salt. Stream in the water, stirring to combine until you get a sticky mixture like thick cake batter. Continue to stir this mixture in one direction with chopsticks for 5 to 7 minutes more to develop the gluten. Cover and let rest at room temperature for 1 to 2 hours.

2 Meanwhile, prepare the fillings, in the order that follows:

To braise the cabbage: Heat a wok over medium heat until just smoking. Ladle in the neutral oil and swirl it around to create a nonstick surface. Add the garlic and fry for 15 to 30 seconds, until fragrant. Add the daikon radish and fry for 1 minute, until the daikon just starts to turn translucent. Add the cabbage and carrot, mixing and tossing for 1 to 2 minutes, until the cabbage just starts to wilt. Stir in the water and salt, bring to a boil, and lower the heat to medium-low or low to maintain

Makes 10 rolls

Popiah Wrappers (makes about 20 wrappers)

4¼ cups (580g) bread flour

2 Tbsp (16g) fine sweet potato starch

¼ cup (24g) wheat germ powder 小麥胚芽粉

1 tsp (6g) salt

2½ cups (600g) water

Braised Cabbage Filling

2 Tbsp neutral oil

3 garlic cloves, sliced

½ medium peeled daikon radish (200g), cut into ¼-inch-thick batons

1 head green cabbage (600g), cut into ¼- to ½-inch-thick strips

1 carrot (100g), cut into thin matchsticks

1½ cups water

1 tsp salt

7 oz (200g) mung bean sprouts

¼ tsp white pepper

1 tsp sesame oil 香油

a slow boil. Cover and braise for 5 to 8 minutes, until the cabbage is softened to your liking. Remove the wok from the heat and add the mung bean sprouts, white pepper, and sesame oil. Toss just until the residual heat wilts the bean sprouts. Set aside for at least 1 hour to allow the flavors to infuse.

To make the red yeast fried pork: Make a lengthwise slit down each gluten intestine and pry them open with your fingers into sheets with lots of exposed nooks and crannies. Using a fork, prick the sheets all over on both sides. In a medium bowl, combine the sugar, red yeast sauce, fermented bean curd, ginger, light soy sauce, rice cooking wine, mushroom powder, and white pepper. Mix well, taste, and season with salt if needed. Place the gluten sheets in the bowl and gently massage the marinade into them. Marinate for at least 30 minutes and up to 2 hours.

3 Prepare a large plate with sweet potato starch. Remove the opened gluten intestines from the marinade, let any excess drip off, and transfer them to the plate. Toss well, taking care to coat all the gluten's crevices. Dust off any excess starch and set aside for at least 5 minutes to hydrate (返潮) the flour.

(continued)

Red Yeast Fried Pork Filling

2 Gluten Intestines 麵腸 (page 58) or use store-bought (200g total)

1 Tbsp golden granulated sugar

2½ Tbsp (50g) red yeast sauce 紅糟

1 small cube (5g) fermented bean curd 豆腐乳, white, red yeast, or sweet wine flavor

1 tsp minced ginger

2 tsp light soy sauce

1 tsp Taiwanese rice cooking wine

(continued)

Popiah Rolls —— continued

4 In a wok over medium-high heat, warm the neutral oil to 340°F (170°C). Fry the gluten sheets for 4 to 5 minutes, flipping halfway through, until both sides are crisp and reddish orange. Transfer to a wire rack to drain and cool. When ready to wrap or serve, chop them into ½-inch-thick strips.

To prepare the bean curd: Rinse and reheat the wok over medium-high heat and swirl in the neutral oil. Add the chopped bean curd and fry for 2 to 3 minutes to release its fragrance. Remove from the wok and set aside.

To make the sha-cha mushrooms: In a large bowl, soak the dried shiitake mushrooms in warm water to cover for 20 to 30 minutes, until fully soft. Drain the mushrooms, reserving the water. Snip off and discard the stems and cut the caps into ¼-inch-thick slices. Rinse and reheat the wok over medium heat and swirl in the neutral oil. Add the mushrooms and fry for 2 to 3 minutes, until fragrant and golden. Add the light soy sauce and a splash of the mushroom soaking water, tossing a few times, until the water has been absorbed. Remove the wok from the heat and stir in the sha-cha sauce and sesame seeds. Season with salt to taste. Mix well, transfer the mushrooms to a plate, and set aside.

To make the curry radish: Rinse and reheat the wok over medium-high heat. Add the preserved radish and fry for 1 to 2 minutes, tossing, until fragrant and the steam dissipates. Transfer the radish to a plate and set aside. Adjust the heat to medium, and swirl in the neutral oil. Add the curry powder and fry for about 30 seconds, until fragrant and foaming. Return the radish to the wok, tossing a few more times to coat it thoroughly. Transfer to a plate and set aside.

5 To cook the wrappers, set a flat and ideally sideless cast-iron griddle over medium-low heat (see Note). Let the pan slowly and evenly heat up. Scoop a portion of the wrapper dough with your fingers (as much as you can hold in your palm), then sling it slightly to get it on the whole surface of your palm.

½ tsp Mushroom Powder 香菇粉 (page 15) or use store-bought

½ tsp white pepper

Salt (optional)

¼ cup (50g) coarse sweet potato starch

About 2 cups neutral oil, for frying

Bean Curd Filling

2 Tbsp neutral oil

14 oz (400g) dark bean curd 黑豆乾/五香豆乾, roughly chopped

Sha-cha Mushrooms Filling

20 dried shiitake mushrooms (60g)

2 Tbsp neutral oil

2 tsp light soy sauce

2 Tbsp vegetarian sha-cha ("barbecue") sauce 素沙茶醬, preferably Bull Head brand 牛頭牌

2 tsp toasted sesame seeds

¼ tsp salt

6 Visualize the pan as a clock. Use ample force to stick the dough in the 7 to 9 o'clock spot, then turn your palm in a clockwise direction to wipe a full circle. When you get to the end, press down hard once and lift the dough up. Quickly use the dough in your palm to tap on any holes or empty spots to fill them and use a scraper to gently flatten any protruding or uneven spots. In 30 to 45 seconds, you should see the popiah turn slightly translucent as the sides start to release. Run a scraper along the sides and gently peel the popiah off the pan. It should release very easily. Flip and cook the other side for about 30 seconds. Transfer to a plate and cover with a damp cloth to keep warm. Wipe the pan clean with a kitchen paper towel to remove any loose crumps and repeat with the remaining 19 pieces, stacking them on top of one another under the damp cloth. You will very likely not get it perfect on the first try, but don't be too hard on yourself! Use the first few popiah to test the heat and technique and build up the confidence.

7 Pour the braised cabbage through a sieve to drain out any excess broth. Don't squeeze the cabbage—having some broth is key to a great rùnbǐng, but having too much will make the popiah too soggy. Place all the fillings within arm's reach.

8 To prepare the popiah rolls, overlap two popiah wrappers by about 2 inches. On a rectangular area in the center, brush on a layer of haishan sauce and add the fillings in this order: chopped cilantro, peanut sugar, powdered sea lettuce, red yeast fried pork, sha-cha mushrooms, bean curd, curry radish, and a mound of braised cabbage. Fold in the sides and roll tightly toward the top, like a burrito. Alternatively, serve all the components separately and let everyone assemble it to their liking at the table.

Curry Radish Filling

4¼ oz (120g) Preserved Radish 菜脯 (page 42), cut into ¼-inch mince

1 Tbsp neutral oil

1 tsp curry powder, preferably S&B brand Golden Curry

-

½ cup Haishan Sauce 海山醬 (page 108)

1 cup roughly chopped cilantro leaves

1 cup Peanut Sugar (page 104)

¼ cup (10g) powdered ulva / sea lettuce 虎苔 or seaweed furikake, or 4 sheets nori blended into a powder

粳米粽 kinn-tsàng

Alkaline Rice Dumplings

These translucent, golden, gelatinous dumplings are a staple of the midsummer Duānwǔjié (端午節, Dragon Boat Festival). As opposed to savory rice dumplings, zòngzi, these are meant to be eaten cold and as snacks. Lye water gives them their distinctive flavor and texture. A-Gong liked his plain and dipped into golden sugar so it had crunchy spikes of sweetness. A-Má loves hers filled with dòushā (Sweet Red Bean Paste, page 245), so I've also included my recipe. If using the bean paste in the filling, roll the paste into golf-ball-size portions. Use less rice to maintain the texture—you should still be able to hear the movement of the rice as you shake the dumpling around.

Makes 20

2½ cups (600g) short-grain (round) sticky/glutinous rice 圓糯米

1 Tbsp (15ml/20g) lye water 粳油

50 dried bamboo leaves 粽葉

Kitchen twine

Sweet Red Bean Paste 紅豆沙 (recipe follows; optional)

Golden granulated sugar, for serving

1 In a medium bowl, rinse the sticky rice three to five times until the water runs mostly clear. Drain and soak with enough water to cover for 2 to 3 hours.

2 Drain the sticky rice, leaving about 2 Tbsp water in the bowl (this will be absorbed by the rice after you add the lye water). Stir in the lye water. The rice should immediately turn a pale yellow color and become a little sticky. Set aside at room temperature for 1 to 2 hours for the rice to absorb the lye water.

3 Rinse and scrub the bamboo leaves. Snip about 1 inch off both ends. (The pointy ends can pierce and break the leaves when wrapping, so snip off just enough to remove them.) In a large, wide pot filled with water, add the trimmed leaves, bring to a boil over high heat, lower the heat to medium-low or low to a gentle boil, and cook for 15 to 20 minutes, until they turn a dark green, to soften the leaves and eliminate any foul odors. Drain and rinse them with cool water and set aside.

4 Using a pair of scissors, cut ten 5-foot segments of kitchen twine. Gather them together, fold them in half, then make a loop knot at the point of

(continued)

Alkaline Rice Dumplings —— continued

the fold. Anchor the loop to a sturdy place (such as a cabinet handle so that you can pull on it to create tension while you wrap).

5 Overlap two bamboo leaves by a little more than half their length, with both leaves' points on each end and the smooth side facing you. (The smooth side doesn't have the protruding central vein.) ❹ Make a small crosswise fold at the center of the overlap, then use the fold to bring in the leaves, creating a funnel-like pocket. Spoon 2 heaping Tbsp of the sticky rice into the pocket. You'll notice that this fills only about 60 percent of the pocket. It's important that you leave room for the rice to expand, otherwise the finished dumplings will be tough.

6 ❺ Hold the pocket loosely with one hand (don't squish it—maintain the same shape before you filled it with rice). ❻ Use your other hand to bring down the top leaves and close the pocket. ❼ Fold the extra tips over to one side and keep folding it over on consecutive sides until the leaf is used up. Secure it with the twine, taking care not to wrap it too tightly (remember, you want to leave room for the rice to grow). ❽ Wrap the twine around the dumpling twice, then make a slipknot so the dumpling can hang on the cabinet handle (or other anchor point).

7 In a large pressure cooker, place the dumplings and fill with enough water to cover. Bring to a boil over high heat, then adjust the heat to medium. Secure the lid and pressure-cook for 30 minutes. Alternatively, you can simmer the dumplings in a covered large pot on the stovetop for about 3 hours.

8 Once the pressure releases, lift out the dumplings using the twine and hang them back on the cabinet handle (or other anchor point), with a large plate or bowl underneath, for 15 to 20 minutes to let the excess water drip out. Transfer to the refrigerator and cool for at least 2 hours before serving. Serve cold, with golden granulated sugar on the side for dipping. Store in an airtight container in the refrigerator for up to 1 week.

豆沙 dòushā | tāu-se

Sweet Red Bean Paste

1 In a small bowl, soak the red beans with enough water to cover by 2 inches for at least 8 hours or overnight.

2 Drain the red beans. In a small pot, add the red beans and enough water to cover. Bring to a boil over high heat, lower to medium-low or low to a gentle boil and cook for 1½ hours until you can easily flatten one between your fingers. Top off the water from time to time to keep the water level above the beans. Drain out the cooking water. Using a slotted spoon, mash the beans until they are mostly smooth with some lumps.

3 In a small nonstick pan over medium to medium-low heat, warm the neutral oil. Add the mashed red beans, dark brown sugar, maltose syrup, and salt. Using a rubber spatula, stir and mix to dissolve the ingredients. Cook the mixture, continuously stirring for 12 to 15 minutes, until you get something that can hold its own, like Play-Doh, and seems dried. It shouldn't stick to your hands when you touch it.

4 Cool and refrigerate in an airtight container for up to 2 weeks or freeze for up to 2 months.

Makes about 2 cups

1¼ cups (250g) red adzuki beans

1 Tbsp neutral oil

½ cup (100g) dark brown sugar 黑糖

2 Tbsp (about 40g) maltose syrup 麥芽糖

Pinch of salt

黑芝麻湯圓 hēizhīmá tāngyuán | oo-muâ-înn-á

Glutinous Rice Balls with Black Sesame

Winter Solstice (Dōngzhì 冬至) is the longest night of the year, and, as per Taiwanese tradition, my family gets together and shares a big pot of tāngyuán. This combination is something my mom remembers fondly. Eating fermented rice is a Chinese tradition for moms in postnatal care. When my A-Má had my mom, my maternal grandpa made her a jar using techniques he brought from his home in Fuzhou. In turn, when my mom gave birth to my brother and me, A-Má made her a jar each time. These tāngyuán are what A-Má cooked with the fermented rice. Their skins are soft and chewy and ooze with warm, nutty black sesame filling. Their black-and-white figure reminds me, as faded photographs do, of the quiet family memories preserved in our food.

1 To make the tāngyuán: In a small bowl, rinse the sticky rice three to five times until the water runs mostly clear. Drain and soak in the 1 cup of water for at least 6 hours and up to overnight. If it is hot outside, refrigerate while soaking—you want the rice to be cold so the blending won't cause it to cook prematurely.

2 Preheat the oven to 355°F (180°C). On two baking trays, spread out the sesame seeds and peanuts separately in a single layer. Roast the sesame seeds for 10 to 12 minutes and the peanuts for 12 to 15 minutes, or until both smell very fragrant and nutty. Set aside to cool. In a blender, blend the sesame seeds, peanuts, and granulated sugar for 3 to 5 minutes, until the natural oils release and the mixture becomes a paste. Transfer the paste into a shallow bowl and freeze for at least 1 hour.

3 Rinse the blender. Add the sticky rice and all its soaking liquid and blend on high for 2 to 4 minutes, until you have a thick, smooth rice slurry. Pour the slurry into a cheesecloth and squeeze the cloth over

Serves 6 to 8

Tāngyuán

1 cup (240g) sticky/glutinous rice 糯米, preferably a 2:1 ratio of short-grain (round) 圓糯米 and long-grain 長糯米

1 cup water

½ cup (75g) raw black sesame seeds

2 Tbsp (25g) unsalted raw, shelled peanuts

¼ cup (50g) golden granulated sugar

Sweet Soup

4 cups water

½ cup (150g) Sweet Fermented Rice 酒釀 (recipe follows)

2 Tbsp (25g) white rock sugar, plus more to taste

(continued)

the sink. **❷** Expel the liquid until you get a pulp that feels like slightly wet chalk.

4 Bring a small pot of water to a boil. Take a tenth of the pulp, or about 30g, and shape it into a ¼-inch-thick disk. **❸** Cook in the gently boiling water for 3 to 5 minutes, until it starts to float and is slightly shiny and translucent. Using a slotted spoon, remove the disk from the water and add it back to the pulp. **❹** Mix and knead in the bowl to incorporate the two until well combined. You should have a dough that is not sticky at all—or just barely sticky. **❺** Now divide the dough into twelve equal portions, about 25g each, and roll each into a ball. Place each rolled ball on a plate as it's shaped and cover with a damp cloth to prevent drying.

5 Remove the chilled filling from the refrigerator and divide it into twelve equal portions, 12g to 13g each.

6 Roll out one ball of dough and into a 2- to 2½-inch disk. **❻** Place a ball of the black sesame paste in the middle, draw up the sides, and pinch the top shut. Repeat for the remaining dough and filling. (I recommend having some dry paper towels on the side, so you can wipe your fingers whenever you have to touch the filling. This way you are less likely to stain and dirty the outer skin of the tāngyuán.)

7 Bring a large pot of water to a boil over high heat. Add all of the tāngyuán, stirring initially to prevent any sticking, lower the heat to medium-low or low, and cook at a slow boil for 8 to 10 minutes, until they float.

8 Meanwhile, make the sweet soup: In a medium pot, bring the water to a boil over high heat. Adjust the heat to low or medium-low to keep the water warm.

9 Using a spider strainer or slotted spoon, transfer the cooked tāngyuán to the medium pot with warm water. Add the sweet fermented rice and rock sugar and taste to adjust the sweetness. The soup should taste just gently sweet, as the tāngyuán themselves are fairly sweet.

10 Ladle the hot soup into serving bowls and serve immediately.

酒釀 jiǔniàng | 酒甘 tsiú-tinn

Sweet Fermented Rice

1 In a medium bowl, rinse the sticky rice once to rid of any dust or impurities. Drain and soak it with enough water to cover for 5 to 6 hours.

2 Line a bamboo steamer with cheesecloth. Drain the sticky rice and add it to the cloth-lined bamboo steamer. Set the steamer over a pot of boiling water and steam on high heat for 15 to 20 minutes, until the grains are translucent and tender.

3 Remove the steamer from the heat and set it over an empty pot. Pour the cold water gradually over the rice to cool it off, allowing the water to flow through and into the pot below, simultaneously using a rice scoop to separate the grains, mix everything, and facilitate cooling. Continue to pour the water until the rice feels slightly cool to the touch, 85° to 95°F (30° to 35°C). Discard the water in the bottom pot.

4 Add the rice wine starter to a ziplock bag. Using a rolling pin, crush the koji into a fine powder. Sprinkle the koji powder over the rice and mix thoroughly.

5 Pack the rice into a lidded 4-cup glass container and use a chopstick to make a well in the center (the well should be deep enough for you to see the bottom glass).

6 Ferment at room temperature for 72 hours. If it's wintertime, wrap the glass container with a blanket or thick towel to keep it warm. About 32 to 48 hours in, you should see lots of liquid (which is sweet rice wine) start filling the container. The initial ferment is complete when the rice unsticks from the interior walls of the container and begins to float as one clumped mass. Move the container to the refrigerator to slow the ferment. It will taste sweeter and sweeter as it ages. Store in the refrigerator for 6 to 12 months.

Makes one 4-cup jar

2¾ cups (500g) short-grain (round) sticky/glutinous rice 圓糯米

About 4 cups cold water, for cooling the rice

½ ball Chinese rice wine starter 酒麴/酒餅 (4g)

Acknowledgments

To A-Gong and A-Má; Mom, Dad, and Kevin; Virgy; family and friends—thank you for everything. To Laurent—this book is nothing without you. To Gemma Tsui, Jade Lu, Slow Chen and team, and Rudy Huang at Siang kháu Lū. To the Nuns at Taipei Dizang Temple. Thanks to Katy Hui-wen Hung for the history lessons.

Index

Note: Page references in *italics* indicate photographs.

A

Apricots
   Almond Tea, *64, 79*

B

Bamboo leaves
   Alkaline Rice Dumplings, *242*, 243–45
Bamboo Shoots
   Bamboo Salad, *128*, 129
   Bamboo Soup, *152*, 153
   Braised, 179
   Buddha Jump over the Wall, 223–24
Bao, Gua, 104–7, *105*
Basil
   -Fragrant Eggplants, 144, *145*
   Preserved Radish Omelet, *186*, 187
   Three Cup Lion's Mane Mushrooms, *194, 195*
Bean Curd. *See also* Tofu
   Fermented, Water Spinach with, 136, *137*
   Popiah Rolls, 238–41, *239*
   and Preserved Greens Stir-Fry, 140, *141*
   Superior Stock, 151
Bean(s), 24. *See also* Soybean(s)
   Mung, Soup with Pearl Barley, 119
   Popcorn Mushrooms, 113–15, *114*
   Sweet Red, and Stewed Peanuts, Tofu Pudding
      with, *120*, 121–22
   Sweet Red, Paste, 245
Beverages
   Almond Tea, *64, 79*
   Black Soybean Milk, 76
   Peanut Rice Milk, *64*, 78
   Soy Milk, 74–76
Bitter Melon and Pineapple Soup, *158*, 159
Black Bean Tofu, 188–90, *189*
Black Soybean Milk, 76
Black vinegar, 14
Blender, 29
Bok choy
   Sesame Noodles, 93–95, *94*
Bread. *See* Flatbread
Buddha Jump over the Wall, 223–24
Burdock root
   Buddha Jump over the Wall, 223–24

C

Cabbage
   Buddha Jump over the Wall, 223–24
   Golden Kimchi, 130–31, *131*
   Herbal Ginger Hot Pot, 209–12, *210*
   Napa, Stew, 191–92, *193*
   Pickled, *102*, 103
   Popiah Rolls, 238–41, *239*
   Pumpkin Fried Rice Noodles, *171*, 196
   Rice, 184, *185*
   Superior Stock, 151
Cashews
   Buddha Jump over the Wall, 223–24
   Four Tonics Soup, 160
   Taiwanese Sticky Rice, 220–22, *221*
Cauliflower and Tomato Stir-Fry, *138*, 139
Chestnuts
   Buddha Jump over the Wall, 223–24
   Taiwanese Sticky Rice, 220–22, *221*
Chili bean paste
   Mala Base, 208
Chilies
   Chili Oil, 95
   Fermented Chili Paste, 16
   Mala Base, 208
Chili flakes
   Chili Oil, 95
Chili Sauce, Sweet, 17
Cinnamon
   Five-Spice, 27
   Thirteen-Spice, 27
Cloves
   Five-Spice, 27
   Thirteen-Spice, 27
Condiments, 10–14
Congee, Sweet Potato, 66, 67
Corn
   Buddha Jump over the Wall, 223–24
   Herbal Ginger Hot Pot, 209–12, *210*
   Popcorn Mushrooms, 113–15, *114*
   Taro Rice Noodle Soup, 165–67, *166*
Cornstarch, 25
Crepes, Egg, *80*, 81
Crullers, Fried, 85–87, *86*
Cucumbers in Sweet Soy Sauce, 47, *48*
Curry Rice, 182–83, *183*

D

Dry goods, 24–25

Dumplings, Alkaline Rice, *242*, 243–45

E

Edamame

Preserved Greens and Bean Curd Stir-Fry, 140, *141*

Eggplants, Basil-Fragrant, 144, *145*

Equipment, 28–29

F

Fennel seeds

Five-Spice, 27

Thirteen-Spice, 27

Fermented Bean Curd

Sweet Wine, 52–53

Water Spinach with, 136, *137*

Fermented Chili Paste, 16

Fermented Mustard Greens, *34*, 35–36

Fermented Rice, Sweet, 249

Fermenting process, 31–32

Festival and food, 215–16

Five-Spice, 27

Flatbread, Sesame, 82–84, *83*

Flours, 25

Food processor, 29

Four Tonics Soup, 160

G

Garlic

Blanched Sweet Potato Leaves, *134*, 135

Pickled, 18

Soy Paste, 101

Ginger

Chili Oil, *95*

Hot Pot, Herbal, 209–12, *210*

Loofah Stir-Fried with, *142*, 143

Winter Melon Soup with Tofu Balls, 156–57

Gluten Intestine

Braised Pork over Rice, 173–75, *174*

Cabbage Rice, 184, *185*

Gua Bao, 104–7, *105*

Popiah Rolls, 238–41, *239*

recipe for, *55*, 58

Soy-Braised Goods, 116–18, *117*

Gluten Puffs

Braised Gluten with Peanuts, *66*, 68

Oyster Omelet, 108–9

recipe for, *55*, 60

Gluten Threads

Braised Pork over Rice, 173–75, *174*

Herbal Ginger Hot Pot, 209–12, *210*

recipe for, *55*, 59

Golden granulated sugar, 10

Gorgon

Four Tonics Soup, 160

Greens. *See also specific greens*

Preserved, *40*, 41

Preserved, and Bean Curd Stir-Fry, 140, *141*

Red Yeast Fried Rice, 180, *181*

Gua Bao, 104–7, *105*

H

Haishan Sauce, 108

Herbal Ginger Hot Pot, 209–12, *210*

Herbs. *See specific herbs*

Holo dialect, 5

Hot Pots

Herbal Ginger, 209–12, *210*

Mala, *204*, 205–8

K

Kimchi, Golden, 130–31, *131*

Koji, 32

Pineapple and Red Yeast Rice Flavor, 53

Pineapple in Soybean Sauce, 50–51, *51*

Sweet Wine Fermented Bean Curd, 52–53

Winter Melon in Soybean Sauce, 45–46, *46*

Kombu, 24

All-Purpose Stock, 150

Mushroom Powder, 15

L

Legumes, 24

Licorice root, dried, 32

Little eats, 96

Loofah Stir-Fried with Ginger, *142*, 143

Lotus Root Soup, 154, *155*

Lotus seeds

Buddha Jump over the Wall, 223–24

Four Tonics Soup, 160

M

Mala Base, 208

Mala Hot Pot, *204*, 205–8

Mandarin Chinese recipe titles, 5

Mee Sua, 168, *169*

Milks

Black Soybean, 76

Peanut Rice, *64*, 78

Soy, 74–76

Monosodium glutamate (MSG), 14

Mung Bean Soup with Pearl Barley, 119

Mung bean sprouts

Popiah Rolls, 238–41, *239*

Sesame Noodles, 93–95, *94*

Mushroom(s)
    All-Purpose Stock, 150
    Beef Noodle Soup, 16–164, *163*
    Bowl Rice Cake, *110*, 111–12
    Braised Gluten with Peanuts, *66*, 68
    Braised Pork over Rice, 173–75, *174*
    Buddha Jump over the Wall, 223–24
    Curry Rice, 182–83, *183*
    dried shiitake, 24
    Five Willow Fried Fish, 197–200, *198*
    Four Tonics Soup, 160
    Herbal Ginger Hot Pot, 209–12, *210*
    Lion's Mane, 62–63, *63*
    Lion's Mane, Three Cup, *194*, 195
    Mee Sua, 168, *169*
    Napa Cabbage Stew, 191–92, *193*
    Oyster Omelet, 108–9
    Popcorn, 113–15, *114*
    Popiah Rolls, 238–41, *239*
    Powder, 15
    Soy-Braised Goods, 116–18, *117*
    Superior Stock, 151
    Taiwanese Sticky Rice, 220–22, *221*
Mustard Greens
    Aged, Minced Pork with, 176–79, *177*
    Fermented, *34*, 35–36
    Gua Bao, 104–7, *105*
    Preserved Greens, *40*, 41
    Soup, Long-Life, *214*, 225
    Sticky Rice Roll, 88–90, *89*
    Stir-Fried, 107

N

Neutral oil, 10
New Year Rice Cake, 231–32, *233*
Noodle(s)
    Mee Sua, 168, *169*
    Napa Cabbage Stew, 191–92, *193*
    Rice, Pumpkin Fried, *171*, 196
    Rice, Taro Soup, 165–67, *166*
    Sesame, 93–95, *94*
    Sesame Oil Vermicelli, 212, *213*
    Soup, Beef, 16–164, *163*
Nuts. *See also specific nuts*
    buying and toasting, 25

O

Oils
    Chili, 95
    neutral, 10
    sesame, 13
    Sesame, Vermicelli, 212, *213*
    toasted sesame, 13
Omelets
    Oyster, 108–9
    Preserved Radish, *186*, 187
Oriental Pickling Melons in White Soy Sauce, *48*, 49

P

Pancakes, Flaky Toon, 91–92
Peanut butter
    Sesame Noodles, 93–95, *94*
Peanut(s)
    Almond Tea, *64*, 79
    Braised Gluten with, *66*, 68
    Gua Bao, 104–7, *105*
    Rice Milk, *64*, 78
    Stewed, and Sweet Red Beans, Tofu Pudding with,
        120, 121–22
Pearl Barley
    Four Tonics Soup, 160
    Mung Bean Soup with, 119
Pickled Cabbage, *102*, 103
Pickled Garlic, 18
Pineapple
    and Bitter Melon Soup, *158*, 159
    and Red Yeast Rice Flavor, 53
    in Soybean Sauce, 50–51, *51*
Plum Pickled Cherry Tomatoes, 132, *133*
Popcorn Mushrooms, 113–15, *114*
Popiah Rolls, 238–41, *239*
Poria
    Four Tonics Soup, 160
Potato(es)
    Curry Rice, 182–83, *183*
    Popcorn Mushrooms, 113–15, *114*
    Sweet, Congee, *66*, 67
Potato starch, 25
Preserved Greens, *40*, 41
Preserved Radish, 42–44, *43*
Preserved vegetables, 30–32
Pudding, Tofu, with Stewed Peanuts and Sweet Red
    Beans, *120*, 121–22
Pumpkin Fried Rice Noodles, *171*, 196
Purple Laver Cake, 115

R

Radish
    Bowl Rice Cake, *110*, 111–12
    Daikon Soup, 157
    Popiah Rolls, 238–41, *239*
    Preserved, 42–44, *43*
    Preserved, Omelet, *186*, 187

Radish, *continued*
    Sticky Rice Roll, 88–90, *89*
    Superior Stock, 151
    Turnip Cake, 234–35
Red Bean(s), Sweet
    Paste, 245
    and Stewed Peanuts, Tofu Pudding with, *120,*
        121–22
Red Yeast (sauce)
    Fried Rice, 180, *181*
    Popiah Rolls, 238–41, *239*
Red Yeast Rice Flavor and Pineapple, 53
Rice
    Balls, Glutinous, with Black Sesame, *246,* 247–49
    Braised Pork over, 173–75, *174*
    Cabbage, 184, *185*
    Cake, Bowl, *110,* 111–12
    cooking, 172
    Curry, 182–83, *183*
    Dumplings, Alkaline, *242,* 243–45
    Milk, Peanut, *64,* 78
    Purple Laver Cake, 115
    Red Yeast Fried, 180, *181*
    for rice cakes, 227
    Sticky, Roll, 88–90, *89*
    Sticky, Taiwanese, 220–22, *221*
    Sweet Fermented, 249
    Sweet Potato Congee, *66, 67*
Rice Cakes
    best rice for, 227
    New Year, 231–32, *233*
    Turnip Cake, 234–35
Rice cooker, 28
Rice cooking wine, 12–13, 32
Rice koji, 32
    Pineapple and Red Yeast Rice Flavor, 53
    Sweet Wine Fermented Bean Curd, 52–53
Rice vinegar, 13
Rock sugar, 11

S

Salad, Bamboo, *128, 129*
Salt, 10, 32
Sauce, Haishan, 108
Seeds. *See also specific seeds*
    buying, 25
    toasting, 25
Sesame oil, 13
Sesame Oil Vermicelli, 212, *213*
Sesame paste
    Sesame Noodles, 93–95, *94*

Sesame seeds
    Glutinous Rice Balls with Black Sesame, *246,*
        247–49
    Sesame Flatbread, 82–84, *83*
Shallots, Fried, 175
Sichuan peppercorns
    Chili Oil, 95
    Five-Spice, 27
    Mala Base, 208
    Thirteen-Spice, 27
Soups
    Bamboo, *152,* 153
    Beef Noodle, 161–64, *163*
    Daikon, 157
    at daily meals, 146
    Four Tonics, 160
    Glutinous Rice Balls with Black Sesame, *246,*
        247–49
    Lotus Root, 154, *155*
    Mee Sua, 168, *169*
    Mung Bean, with Pearl Barley, 119
    Mustard Greens, Long-Life, *214,* 225
    Pineapple and Bitter Melon, *158,* 159
    Taro Rice Noodle, 165–67, *166*
    Winter Melon, with Tofu Balls, 156–57
Soybean koji, 32
    Pineapple in Soybean Sauce, 50–51, *51*
    Sweet Wine Fermented Bean Curd, 52–53
    Winter Melon in Soybean Sauce, 45–46, *46*
Soybean(s)
    Black, Milk, 76
    Black Bean Tofu, 188–90, *189*
    Preserved Greens and Bean Curd Stir-Fry, 140, *141*
    Soy Milk, 74–76
Soybean sprouts
    All-Purpose Stock, 150
Soy Chicken
    recipe for, 61, *61*
    Soy-Braised Goods, 116–18, *117*
Soy Milk, 74–76
Soy Milk, Savory, *64,* 77
Soy Sauce
    black bean white, 12
    dark, 12
    light, 11–12
    paste, 12
    Paste, Garlic, 101
    Soy-Braised Goods, 116–18, *117*
    Sweet, Cucumbers in, 47, *48*
    White, Oriental Pickling Melons in, *48,* 49

Spices, 26–27. *See also specific spices*
    Five-Spice, 27
    making a braising pouch with, 26
    making a powder with, 26
    Thirteen-Spice, 27
Spring Festival, 215–16
Squash
    Golden Kimchi, 130–31, *131*
    Pumpkin Fried Rice Noodles, *171*, 196
Star anise
    Five-Spice, 27
    Thirteen-Spice, 27
Starches, 25
Stew, Napa Cabbage, 191–92, *193*
Sticky Rice, Taiwanese, 220–22, *221*
Sticky Rice Roll, 88–90, *89*
Stocks
    All-Purpose, 150
    Superior, 151
    in Taiwanese cooking, 146
Sugar, 10, 11, 32
Swatow mustard
    Fermented Mustard Greens, *34*, 35–36
    Long-Life Mustard Greens Soup, *214*, 225
Sweet Chili Sauce, 17
Sweet Potato(es)
    Congee, *66*, 67
    Leaves, Blanched, *134*, 135
    Popcorn Mushrooms, 113–15, *114*
Sweet potato starch, 25

T
Taiwanese recipe titles, 5
Taro
    Balls, Fried, *236*, 237
    Rice Noodle Soup, 165–67, *166*
Textured vegetable protein (TVP)
    Minced Pork with Aged Mustard Greens, 176–79, *177*
Thirteen-Spice, 27
Toasted sesame oil, 13
Tofu
    Balls, Winter Melon Soup with, 156–57
    Black Bean, 188–90, *189*
    Buddha Jump over the Wall, 223–24
    Herbal Ginger Hot Pot, 209–12, *210*
    Mala Hot Pot, *204*, 205–8
    Pudding with Stewed Peanuts and Sweet Red Beans, *120*, 121–22

Soy-Braised Goods, 116–18, *117*
Sweet Wine Fermented Bean Curd, 52–53
Taro Rice Noodle Soup, 165–67, *166*
Tofu skin paste
    Preserved Radish Omelet, *186*, 187
Tofu skin rolls
    Crispy Fried Tofu Skin, 101–3, *102*
    Egg Crepes, *80*, 81
    Five Willow Fried Fish, 197–200, *198*
    Napa Cabbage Stew, 191–92, *193*
    Oyster Omelet, 108–9
    Soy-Braised Goods, 116–18, *117*
    Soy Chicken, 61, *61*
Tofu skin sheets, dried
    Soy Chicken, 61, *61*
Tomato(es)
    and Cauliflower Stir-Fry, *138*, 139
    Cherry, Plum Pickled, 132, *133*
    Superior Stock, 151
Tools, 28
Toon Pancakes, Flaky, 91–92
Traditional Chinese medicine (TCM), 202

V
Vegetables, 126–27. *See also specific vegetables*
    Mala Hot Pot, *204*, 205–8
    preserved, 30–32
    stir-frying, 126–27
Vegetarian meat, about, 54
Vinegar, black, 14
Vinegar, rice, 13
Vital Wheat Gluten, 57

W
Water caltrope
    Lotus Root Soup, 154, *155*
Water Spinach with Fermented Bean Curd, 136, *137*
Wheat Gluten. *See also* Gluten Intestine; Gluten Puffs; Gluten Threads
    recipe for, *55*, 56–57
White pepper, 11
Winter Melon
    Bamboo Soup, *152*, 153
    Soup with Tofu Balls, 156–57
    in Soybean Sauce, 45–46, *46*
Woks, 28–29

Y
Yam
    Four Tonics Soup, 160

Typefaces: Jean François Porchez's Sabon Next and Monotype's MSungHK

Library of Congress Cataloging-in-Publication Data
Names: Lee, George, 2001- author.
Title: A-Gong's table : vegan recipes from a Taiwanese home / George Lee ;
    photography by Laurent Hsia.
Description: California : Ten Speed Press, [2024] | "A Chez Jorge Cookbook."
Identifiers: LCCN 2022055882 (print) | LCCN 2022055883 (ebook) | ISBN
    9781984861276 (trade paperback) | ISBN 9781984861283 (ebook)
Subjects: LCSH: Cooking, Chinese—Taiwan style. | Vegan cooking. |
    LCGFT: Cookbooks.
Classification: LCC TX724.5.C5 L4454 2024 (print) | LCC TX724.5.C5
    (ebook) | DDC 641.5951—dc23/eng/20221128
LC record available at https://lccn.loc.gov/2022055882
LC ebook record available at https://lccn.loc.gov/2022055883

Trade Paperback ISBN: 978-1-9848-6127-6
eBook ISBN: 978-1-9848-6128-3

Printed in Malaysia

Acquiring editor: Emma Rudolph | Project editor: Claire Yee
Production editor: Patricia Shaw
Design: Mistroon | Deputy creative director: Emma Campion
Production designers: Mari Gill and Mara Gendell
Production manager and prepress color manager: Jane Chinn
Food stylist: George Lee | Food stylist assistant: Slow Chen
Prop stylist: Gemma Tsui
Copy editor: Kathy Brock | Proofreader: Liana Faughnan
Indexer: Elizabeth T. Parson
Publicist: Lauren Chung | Marketer: Monica Stanton

10 9 8 7 6 5 4 3 2 1

First Edition